The Play-By-Play Guide

to

Be A College Athlete

By Mary A. Wegzyn

Play-by-Play Guides
Knoxville, Tennessee

For updates and more information,
Go to www.BeACollegeAthlete.com
Or on Twitter follow
@BeACollegeAth

Representatives are available to speak to schools, clubs, and
groups. To schedule a presentation, contact

Email: BeACollegeAthlete@AOL.com

Printed in the United States of America
First printing, 2007

**This publication is designed with the intent of providing accurate information with
regard to the subject matter covered. It is sold with the understanding that neither
the author nor the publisher are engaged in rendering legal or other professional
services regarding the subject matter covered. If legal or other expert advice is
desired, the services of a competent professional should be sought.**

TABLE OF CONTENTS

Introduction

Playing a sport at the college level is something people dream about. Those who played at the college level are few. Often they are looked at as the elite, because those individuals were able to continue playing their sport when the majority of their peers were not. Everyone assumes that those who play at the next level are the best of the best, the stars of the all-stars. But this is not the reality.

In 1982 I was party to a conversation with the father of NFL pro-bowl player Steve Buerlein, who at the time was completing his senior year at Servite High School in Southern California. Mr. Buerlein expressed his excitement and his exasperation with all the attention his son was receiving from college recruiters and the media. Mr. Buerlein shared that the recruiting process was somewhat overwhelming for him and his family. He said something that I have never forgotten. Mr. Buerlein said that he was unprepared for the entire college recruiting process -- there were no books on the topic and no guides to help an athlete get through the procedures. The fact that this Blue Chip athlete and his family were unprepared for the events surrounding college recruiting made me wonder how average players managed to muddle their way through the process.

As a parent, I have attended many of my kids' sporting events. While sitting in the stands I've heard parents talk among themselves about a student-athlete's talents and skills. Parents usually put themselves in one of two categories. The first is the "My kid is so great that colleges will be knocking down our door to sign her/him." The second is the "No one on this team has a chance of playing college sports." Through the years, I've listened as parents discuss their shock that the star of some team didn't go on to play a sport in college and yet one or two of the less talented team members did. The general feeling is there was no rhyme or reason why one kid has the opportunity to play a sport in college while another does not. The whole college recruitment and scholarship process, to many people, is a great mystery. This really disturbs me because something so important should not be shrouded in such mystery.

As the mother of four athletic sons, and the wife of a former NCAA D1 athlete, I realized I might need to learn as much as possible about the college recruiting process. I decided to delve into the topic of college athletic scholarships and recruiting. I spent sixteen dedicated weeks searching out and reading everything I could find on the topic. I was surprised to learn only a dozen or so books existed on this subject, and some of the best books were self-published. Clearly there was a lack of information for parents and student-athletes and a need for a means of education about the process. I continued researching this topic.

My continued research led me to attend some high school presentations given by experts in the areas of college sports recruitment or NCAA eligibility. The more seminars and presentations I attended, the more I realized I knew about the subject. I was surprised that these "experts" weren't saying anything I didn't already know, and I was shocked when they were unable to answer questions to which I knew the answers!

In the meantime, I helped my friends' kids through the recruiting process. I loaned out materials, gave suggestions and advice on the best ways to market student-athletes, and I proofread profiles. After walking enough people through the process and watching their successes, I knew it was time to write this book and begin giving my own presentations. I had to "take my show on the road" to help others demystify this process. Something this important shouldn't be such a mystery.

In 2008 my oldest son, Matthew, graduated high school. During his high school career we began using for ourselves the techniques and systems I had created. I had already helped so many other student-athletes use this system with great success, and we were pleased to see how well the techniques worked! After much interest by numerous schools, Matthew landed at the University of Tennessee and played D1 football as a Volunteer from 2008 – 2011. Matthew graduated with a degree in Journalism/Broadcasting/Communications in 2012. He has now partnered with his former teammate and friend, Derrick Furlow, to help others learn how to get recruited, like they were.

My next son, Michael, graduated high school in 2011. By the start of his junior year of high school, he was already being steadily recruited for football as a quarterback. Our family relocated from Michigan to Tennessee in the middle of his junior year of high school and I was afraid colleges might lose interest in him due to the move. We also had the daunting task of finding a high school that ran a pro-style offense and needed a new starting quarterback. My fears proved to be unfounded when, a mere two months after moving to Tennessee, Mike was named the number one quarterback in the state. Even though he had not yet played a down, thrown a pass, or taken a snap (he was playing Varsity basketball at the time) in the state of Tennessee, his recruiting profile followed him. Mike was awarded a D1 athletic scholarship to the University of Massachusetts where he red-shirted his first year and started the next two. He managed to graduate in three years, and he will play his last two years of eligibility for the University of Tennessee football team and earn his Master's Degree.

I sincerely hope you find the information in this book useful in your quest to participate in college athletics. I always welcome feedback from readers and people who have attended my seminars.

Best of luck to you!

Mary

Photo by Steve Fecht

"...No man can be a football player who does not love the game. Half-heartedness or lack of earnestness will eliminate any man from a football team. The love of the game must be genuine. It is not devotion to a fad that makes men play football; it is because they enjoy their struggle."

Fielding H. Yost

Chapter 1

Why Play College Sports?

So you think you want to play college sports. Why? Before you start this endeavor, examine your reasons for wanting to do this. College student-athletes have multiple demands on their time and energy that other students do not. Twenty percent of all student-athletes who begin their college careers participating in collegiate sports end up quitting the sport prior to graduation. Why? Some get injured, some become academically ineligible, and some find out they can't be competitive at this level. Unfortunately, others quit because of burn out and an inability or unwillingness to juggle all the demands of school and sport.

Student-athletes have many reasons for wanting to continue playing their sport at the collegiate level. Some of the more common reasons follow:

- **The Love** - This is an out-and-out love for the sport. Participation in the sport has been a part of the student-athlete's life for years and not participating is unimaginable.
- **Time Limit** - There is a small window of opportunity in life to compete in most sports.
- **Physical Fitness** – While participating in college athletics, student-athletes maintain training schedules and regimens that often result in a better level of physical fitness.
- **Time Management** – A number of student-athletes find they are more successful in the classroom during the season than they are during the off-season. Participation in a sport demands a huge time commitment.

Student-athletes have less free time and often tend to use their time wisely when in season.

- **Money** – Student-athletes hope to receive financial aid to pay for college via their participation in athletics.
- **Social Circles** – Incoming freshmen find an immediate circle of friends when part of a team. College campuses can be big places, and it is nice to know people who have common interests.

All of these reasons are fine, but the goal really is to get an education. Higher education results in higher lifetime earnings. A college degree increases earning potential by more than one million dollars over the course of a lifetime. If participation in a sport can bring needed funds to pay for a college education, the benefits can last a lifetime.

The NCAA's Director of Public and Media Relations, Erik Christianson, announced in a press release November 9, 2006, student-athletes' graduation rates exceeded those of the general student body. Of student-athletes entering Division I schools in 1999, an impressive 77% graduated within a six-year period. That is 14 points higher than the national graduation rates of the general student body at these schools in the same time period. At NCAA Division II schools, 69% of students who participated in college athletics and entered college in 1999 completed their degrees, versus 46% of those in the general student body.

Why is this? The answer is simple. College student-athletes are competitive and driven. They are results oriented. They like to win. College student-athletes have disciplined schedules, the support of coaches (who often become on-campus parent figures), and access to team study-tables and tutoring. College coaches have support systems in place for the student-athlete. The non-student-athlete must forage through the system to learn about and take advantage of these support systems.

To begin the process to play college athletics, the first thing every student-athlete and parent needs to do is request a free copy of the NCAA and NAIA Guide for the College-Bound Student-Athlete. This brochure, published annually in November for the coming year, guides you through the most basic steps to progress from a high school athlete to a college athlete. Request a copy every year your student is in high school in order to stay on top of rule changes.

Important Free Guide

One of the best resources available for high school student-athletes who have any thought of playing their sport in college is free and is revised annually. The "Guide for the College-Bound Student-Athlete" should be obtained each and every year of a student-athlete's high school career. This publication is available from the two major governing bodies of college athletics, the National College Athletic Association (NCAA) and the National Association of Intercollegiate Athletics (NAIA). In these guides you will find up-to-the-minute information about conference eligibility requirements regarding academics and amateurism. Also in these guides will be definitions of basic recruiting terms as well as general information about the rules and dates college coaches must follow when contacting a student-athlete.

These free guides may be viewed on a computer as a pdf file, obtained via a download from the conference's website, or by calling the conference office and requesting it be mailed to your home.

NCAA Eligibility Center
Print, Download, or Call for the
"Guide for the College-Bound Student-Athlete"
The website is: www.ncaa.org.
Toll-free phone number for U.S. callers is 877-262-1492
Phone number for international callers is 317-223-0700
Customer service hours are 10 a.m. to 5 p.m. Eastern time, Monday through Friday
The NCAA offices are located in Indianapolis, IN

NAIA Eligibility Center

View the pdf file entitled:

"Guide   for   the   College-Bound   Student-Athlete"
www.playnaia.org/d/NAIA_GuidefortheCollegeBoundStudent.pd

Website: playNAIA.org

Contact the NAIA by Phone, Fax & Email:

Phone: 816-595-8300

Toll free: 866-881-6242

Fax: 816-595-8301

Email: ecinfo@naia.org

International student questions, contact: ecinternational@naia.org

Customer Service Hours are Monday through Friday 8:30 a.m. to 5 p.m. Central Time

The NAIA offices are located in Kansas City, MO

Notes

Photo by Steve Fecht

"Always make a total effort, even when the odds are against you."

Arnold Palmer

Chapter 2

Where to Play College Sports?

One of the most important concepts that parents and student-athletes need to understand is this: **The student-athlete will not choose the school; the school will choose the student-athlete.**

Common Mistakes

Student-athletes and their parents often have a set of ideals regarding where the student-athlete will play. Many of these are unrealistic, and most of these limit the opportunities available to the student-athlete.

Often, student-athletes and parents set their sites on the big schools, the "name" schools, the schools who are perennial participants in the big college bowl games. No one should ever be discouraged from the goal and the dream of playing at these schools, but it is important for the dream to be kept in perspective. These big-name schools have first pick of all the high school athletic and academic talent due to the exposure they receive from the media, through national sponsorship contracts, and the universities' licensing agreements with makers of apparel, gift items, etc. Many student-athletes want to attend these schools. The competition is fierce. If a student-athlete sets his or her heart on playing for one of these schools, chances are the student-athlete will be disappointed. Even if a student-athlete is talented enough to play at that level, the school may not be recruiting players for the student-athlete's particular position. Student-athletes should certainly contact their favorite school or schools, but all other options need to be explored as well. Remember, student-athletes must not limit choices only to big-name schools;

83% of the opportunities to compete at the college level are outside of Division I NCAA sports.

Student-athletes and parents also limit opportunities by only considering schools within certain geographic perimeters. Often, it is decided that the student-athlete only will consider schools within a particular drive-time radius of his or her hometown. Parents decide on a maximum number of travel hours from home that they are willing to travel and then look at all schools within that area. The problem with this method of selection is that it eliminates more schools than it includes. The best opportunity, the best "fit," and the best educational and athletic experience for the student-athlete may very well be outside of this area. Rather than limit your student-athlete to a three-hour drive-time radius, perhaps you should expand your area to a three-hour fly-time radius. The idea is to keep open as many options as possible.

Due to the daunting cost of non-resident tuition, many student-athletes eliminate all out-of-state schools. This is a very common mistake that, again, limits the student-athlete's opportunities. One element that may make a student-athlete attractive to an out-of-state school is that out-of-state residents help colleges' and universities' diversity percentages. Every college and university strives to enroll students from all 50 states. Your student-athlete might be the only person on campus from your state. Suddenly, your student-athlete is much more valuable to the campus community and may be eligible for even more scholarship money. Again, try not to rule out any schools, especially early in the process.

Things to Consider

Again, keep in mind, the school ultimately will choose the student-athlete. Not every school needs an athlete in every position every recruiting year. Coaches have depth charts, and they recruit athletes to fill vacancies on those depth charts. One way to get an idea whether or not a school would consider recruiting your student-athlete is to look at the current roster. How many athletes are rostered at your student-athlete's position? Of those athletes, how many are upper-classmen? If your student-athlete is a center on a basketball team and the school he or she hopes to attend has two freshman centers and a sophomore center on the roster, chances are the coach won't be recruiting heavily for another center for a couple of years.

Certain schools do not recruit athletes for certain positions. For years the University of Michigan football program did not recruit players as kickers. The kicker was usually a walk-on player or a player who was recruited for another position and also happened to kick. If a student-athlete specialized in place kicking or punting, the University of Michigan would not contact him. This type of information is vitally important for a student-athlete to know if he or she has his or her heart set on playing at a certain school and that school does not recruit for that position.

If a school needs to recruit a player for a specific position, the recruiting coach does not consider only one prospective student-athlete for the position -- many student-athletes are recruited for that one position. The recruiting coach prioritizes those recruits on a recruiting depth chart. If the school's first choice recruit decides to attend another school, the coach then moves to the second choice recruit, and so on. A student-athlete has no way of knowing what spot he or she holds on the recruiting depth chart. It is recommended that the student-athlete politely, but bluntly, ask the coach where they are on the depth chart. Some coaches may not divulge this information because it takes away their advantage in the recruiting and bargaining process, but some coaches will share this information. It doesn't hurt to ask! The top five athletes on a school's depth chart will be invited on "official" campus visits and be treated like VIPs. If the first choice recruit commits to the school, the other four recruits who were the second, third, fourth, and fifth choices and were treated like 'gold' up until that time will not get an offer from that school. Remember, the school chooses the student-athlete; the student-athlete does not choose the school. This is one more reason to keep all options open and not reject a school until it rejects your student-athlete or the student-athlete has completely investigated and considered what it might have to offer.

Photo by R. Grant

"The difference between a successful person and others is not a lack of strength, not a lack of knowledge, but rather a lack of will."

Vincent T. Lombardi

Chapter 3

College Athletic Associations

Seven main collegiate athletic associations govern sports at universities and colleges in the United States and Canada. They are the NCAA, NAIA, NJCAA, NCCAA, USCAA, CIA, and CCAA. Each of these athletic associations has a unique focus, slightly different philosophies, and its own set of eligibility standards. Although the NCAA has the most member institutions, it is important to remember this it is not the only governing body in college athletics. Other college athletic associations represent significant numbers of schools. If the goal is to play a sport at the college level and to attempt to get funding for a college education through participation in a sport, all of these athletic associations should receive consideration from student-athletes.

NCAA

www.ncaa.org

When most people think of college athletics, they think of the NCAA (National Collegiate Athletic Association). In 2007, the NCAA entered its second century as a governing body for college athletics. With over 1,200 member schools and more than 444,000 student-athletes who combine education and athletics at these schools, the NCAA is usually the first college athletic association that comes to mind. In the last decade the number of student-athletes participating in sports at NCAA has more than doubled.

The NCAA schools are divided into three divisions - Division I, Division II, and Division III. In the sport of football, Division I schools are subdivided into FBS, Football Bowl Subdivision (formerly Division I-A) and FCS, Football Championship Subdivision (formerly Division I-AA). With regard to scholarships, each division and subcategory of each division are governed by different NCAA regulations. In 2012, there were over 110,586 scholarships available at NCAA member institutions. Schools in NCAA Division III are not allowed to offer any money based on a student's athletic ability, which does not mean that financial aid is not awarded to student-athletes.

In order to participate in athletics at an NCAA member school, a student-athlete must register with the NCAA Eligibility Center (formerly known as the NCAA Clearinghouse). Registration should be started after the student-athlete's first varsity season. Be sure to consult with the student-athlete's high school counselor regarding core course requirements to be eligible to compete at an NCAA school. Strict attention is needed to the student-athlete's high school course selection in order to assure the student-athlete will be eligible to play in the NCAA. If even one part of the requirement for eligibility is not met, the student-athlete will be declared ineligible. Just because everything appears to be moving along smoothly does not mean the student-athlete will be declared eligible. There is a long list of student-athletes who have graduated high school, moved onto campus, and are living in a college dorm who are declared ineligible. If that happens, the student-athlete will not be allowed to practice or be a part of the college team in any way. The best way to be certain the NCAA will declare a student-athlete eligible is to follow the guidelines in the free guide, the <u>NCAA Guide for the College-Bound Student-Athlete</u>, and to meet regularly with the student-athlete's high school counselor. Keep in mind, not all high school courses qualify as core courses!

TOTAL AVAILABLE NCAA ATHLETIC SCHOLARSHIPS – MEN & WOMEN

	Men - D1	Men - D1	Men - D3	Total Men's Sports
Baseball	297	266	375	938
Basketball	346	312	415	1073
Bowling	1	0	0	1
Cross Country	315	267	394	976
Equestrian				
Fencing	20	2	12	34
Field Hockey				
Football	246	167	242	655
(I-FBS 120)				
(I-FCS 126)				
Golf	298	231	281	810
Gymnastics	16	0	1	17
Ice Hockey	59	6	73	138
Lacrosse	62	50	205	317
Rifle	4	0	1	5
Rowing	28	3	29	60
Rugby				
Sand Volleyball				
Soccer	204	206	407	817
Softball				
Swimming & Diving	136	67	214	417
Tennis	262	176	331	769
Track & Field, Indoor	263	137	248	648
Track & Field, Outdoor	283	181	279	743
Volleyball	23	19	64	106
Water Polo	22	7	14	43
Wrestling	78	54	88	220

	Women D1	Women D2	Women D3	Total Women's Sports
Basketball	344	314	438	1096
Bowling	35	19	8	72
Cross Country	343	295	417	1055
Equestrian	18	4	16	38
Fencing	23	3	15	41
Field Hockey	79	27	161	267
Golf	260	173	187	620
Gymnastics	62	7	15	84
Ice Hockey	34	3	50	88
Lacrosse	96	75	239	410
Rifle	8	1	1	10
Rowing	88	18	41	147
Rugby	2	1	2	5
Sand Volleyball	20	1	0	21
Soccer	322	258	433	1013
Softball	289	289	412	990
Swimming & Diving	196	87	249	532
Tennis	321	238	379	939
Track & Field, Indoor	315	160	254	729
Track & Field, Outdoor	323	202	289	814
Volleyball	329	300	430	1059
Water Polo	33	12	16	61

NAIA

www.naia.com

The NAIA (National Association of Intercollegiate Athletics) has more than 300 member colleges and universities in the United States and Canada. It was established in 1937 in Kansas City, MO. More than 90% of these member universities offer athletic scholarships to the more than 60,000 student-athletes who compete in 13 men's and women's sports at the Division I and II level. The NAIA holds 23 national championships each year. In order to compete at the NAIA level, a student-athlete must register with the NAIA Eligibility Center. The NAIA Guide for the College-Bound Student-Athlete is available online at the NAIA.com website. It is advisable for student-athletes and their parents to be familiar with the requirements of eligibility. The **maximum** number of scholarships offered **per sport per school** follows.

SPORT	Division I	Division II
Baseball	12	
Basketball (Men)	11	6
Basketball (Women)	11	6
Football	24	
Golf (Men)	5	
Golf (Women)	5	
Soccer (Men)	12	
Soccer (Women)	12	
Softball	10	
Swimming & Diving	8	
Tennis (Men)	5	
Tennis (Women)	5	
Track & C.C. (Men)	12	5
Track & C.C. (Women)	12	5
Volleyball (Women)	8	
Wrestling	8	

NJCAA

www.njcaa.org

The NJCAA (National Junior College Athletic Association) is the governing body of intercollegiate athletics for two-year colleges. It was established in 1938 and recently celebrated its 75th anniversary. It is headquartered in Colorado Springs, CO.

The NJCAA has 500+ member schools where more than 50,000 student-athletes participate in 15 men's and 13 women's sports. Student-athletes who plan to participate in a sport at a two-year school sign a NJCAA National Letter of Intent. Eligibility for competition varies by school. Student-athletes are allowed two seasons of participation. Student-athletes must be full-time students.

Junior college can be a great option for student-athletes. There is a perception that only student-athletes who do not qualify or are ineligible to attend a four-year college or university attend a junior college, but that is not true. For example, baseball players often opt to play at the junior college level because 500+ schools have baseball teams. There are only 298 NCAA D1 schools with baseball programs, so the opportunity to play at the JUCO level is greater. At the end of two years of junior college, many student-athletes plan to transfer to a four-year school to finish out their full four years of athletic eligibility. If this is the plan, it is wise to take a look at the rosters of the desired four-year school to see which junior colleges the current players have transferred from. Certain two-year schools tend to feed into particular four-year schools.

The NJCAA is divided into regions and holds 47 national championships each year and participates in 8 football bowl games. The member schools are divided into Divisions I, II, and III. Division I schools offer full athletic scholarships that include tuition, fees, room, board, books, course related materials, and transportation costs one time per academic year to and from college by the most direct route. Division II schools' athletic scholarships are limited to full tuition, fees and books, while Division III schools give no athletically related financial assistance. The **maximum** number of athletic scholarships at NJCAA schools in the following sports is listed.

MEN	WOMEN
Baseball – 24	Basketball – 16
Basketball – 16	Golf – 8
Football – 85	Ice Hockey – 16
Golf – 8	Lacrosse – 20
Ice Hockey – 16	Soccer – 18
Lacrosse – 20	Softball – 24
Soccer – 18	Tennis – 8
Tennis – 8	Track & C.C. – 30
Track & C.C. – 30	Volleyball – 14
Water Polo – 4.5	Water Polo – 8
Wrestling – 16	

NCCAA

www.theNCCAA.org

The NCCAA (National Christian College Athletic Association) is a Christ-based governing body of college athletics. It was established in 1968 and is headquartered in Greenville, SC. Member schools total over 100 and are divided into Division I and Division II categories in eight regions. The schools are usually small Christian liberal arts and bible study colleges and universities. The NCCAA provides 15,000+ student-athletes with athletic financial aid at its member schools. Twenty-five national championship events and several invitational tournaments are sponsored by the NCCAA. Christian Service Projects (CSPs) are held during every championship and invitational in the host community. Each individual school's athletic director decides eligibility of student-athletes. To learn more about this conference and to find a list of schools and coach's contact information, go to: http://www.thenccaa.org/custompages/2013-14%20Membership%20Directory.pdf. The number of **member institutions** that have participation in each sport follows.

SPORT	Division I	Division II
Baseball	59	18
Basketball (Men)	66	41
Basketball (Women)	64	33
Cross Country (Men)	56	17
Cross Country (Women)	58	18
Football	18	2
Golf (Men)	47	9
Golf (Women)	36	3
Indoor Track and Field (M)	36	3
Indoor Track and Field (W)	37	--
Lacrosse	6	1
Soccer (Men)	63	29
Soccer (Women)	61	18
Softball	35	9
Swimming	6	---
Tennis (Men)	37	3
Tennis (Women)	40	4
Track and Field (Men)	41	3
Track and Field (Women)	42	3
Volleyball (Men)	4	4
Volleyball (Women)	61	38
Wrestling	6	1

USCAA

www.theUSCAA.com

The USCAA (United States Small Collegiate Athletic Association) is an organization of more than 100 small-school athletic programs. The USCAA provides small colleges the opportunity to compete against other small colleges. This provides other small colleges the opportunity to compete for National Championships versus colleges of like size and resources. The USCAA Basketball National Championships is one of the larger tournaments in college athletics featuring 34 teams playing in two men's and women's divisions.

Members of the USCAA (formerly known as the NSCAA) are accredited schools of higher learning with similar enrollment numbers. Each institution offers varying types of degrees. "Small college" translates to total enrollment at these institutions of between 500 and 2000 students.

The USCAA has eligibility and compliance rules that are similar to the NCAA and NAIA. Some of the USCAA schools have a dual affiliation with the NAIA, NCCSA, and NCAA Division III. The USCAA supports six men's sports as well as five women's sports in two divisions.

CCAA

www.ccaa.ca

The Canadian Collegiate Athletic Association is the governing body of college athletics in Canada. The CCAA was established in 1971 but officially founded in 1974 and is headquartered is in Cornwall, Ontario. Seven sports are supported at ten national championships. There are 100+ member institutions consisting of colleges, universities, technical institutes, and cegeps. (A cegep is a vocational school in Quebec). All members are divided into five conferences.

Attending school in Canada is a very real opportunity for American student-athletes and it isn't far geographically from states in the northern areas of the U.S. The CCAA is celebrating its 40th year in existence during the 2014-2015 athletic season.

Competition for both men and women is available in the following sports:

Badminton
Basketball
Cross Country
Curling
Golf
Soccer
Volleyball

CIS

www.cis-sic.ca

The Canadian Interuniversity Sport is another governing body over college athletics in Canada. There are 56 member schools divided into four regions. CIS represents 11,000 student-athletes who may compete in 21 national championships in twelve sports.

Basketball (men's & women's)
Cross Country (men's & women's)
Curling (men's & women's)
Field Hockey (women's)
Football (men's)
Ice Hockey (men's & women's)
Rugby (women's)
Soccer (men's & women's)
Swimming (men's & women's)
Track and Field (men's & women's)
Volleyball (men's and women's)
Wrestling (men's and women's)

Notes

Photo by Steve Fecht

"If you put in the work, the results will come."
Michael Jordan

Chapter 4

Why You Need to Market A Student-Athlete

Even a student-athlete of average talent and athletic ability can participate in college athletics. There is a college where the student-athlete should be able to play his or her sport. Although no coaches ever contact some student-athletes, there are schools and coaches who would have loved to have those student-athletes play for them if only the coaches knew about the student-athlete or had the budget to find and recruit the student-athlete. Marketing is one of the least understood components of the recruiting process. Often, student-athletes and parents have no idea why college coaches contact some student-athletes and other student-athletes are not contacted at all. The most important concept for student-athletes and parents to grasp is that **full responsibility for marketing a student-athlete belongs to the people who have the most to gain** – the student-athlete and the student-athlete's parents.

Student-athletes and their parents must be proactive in the recruiting process. Student-athletes and their parents need to send profiles to a minimum of 70 schools – ideally, profiles should be sent to at least 100 schools. At least 25 of these should be sent to schools in Division II and 25 to schools in Division III. Member schools of each of the various athletic associations should be contacted. Profiles should be sent to schools that are large and schools that are small. It is important to remember that participating in a program in a less competitive division or at a smaller school is no less enjoyable than at a well-known Division I school, but the focus and opportunities may be different. Statistics prove, the more darts you throw at a target, the greater your odds of scoring a bulls-eye – marketing a student-athlete to college programs should reflect this same law of statistics. It is not unreasonable to contact more than 300 schools nationwide.

Common Misconceptions

If you are good enough – they will find you!

One of the most common misconceptions is "if you are good enough, they will find you". Most people believe a student-athlete capable of playing at the next level will be discovered or randomly contacted by college coaches. This is absolutely not true. Many student-athletes who would be an asset to most college athletic programs are unknown to 99% of the college coaches in their own state and certainly unknown to college coaches across the country. It is impossible for a college coach to contact a student-athlete that the college coach does not know about. If college coaches do not contact a student-athlete by the sophomore year of high school, there is a good chance that student-athlete may never be contacted. Student-athletes and student-athletes' parents must be proactive. Student-athletes need to be marketed to colleges.

To completely understand this, it is important to understand what a college coach's job entails. College coaches have an obligation to coach a team. If the team does not have a winning season, the coach can lose his or her job. The coach's first priority is coaching. Recruiting is a part of a coach's job that many do not enjoy, and some actually find repugnant. Bo Schembechler, legendary coach of the University of Michigan football team, often said he hated recruiting because it made him feel like a pimp. Head coaches, like Bo, delegate the brunt of recruiting responsibilities to an assistant coach. These coaches have certain sources they reference to get names of student-athletes that may be of interest to the college. If a student-athlete's name is not in front of a coach, the coach does not have the time, budget, or resources to find other prospects. Student-athletes who market themselves to college programs have the advantage of having their name in front of the recruiting coach.

The high school or club coach is going to get a student-athlete recruited by colleges.

Another fallacy is that the student-athlete's high school coach or club coach is mostly responsible for marketing the student-athlete to college programs.

The coach is usually the first person blamed if a student-athlete does not receive enough letters or visits from college coaches. Yet, few high school coaches or club coaches in the country have the time, budget, contacts, or knowledge to properly market even one student-athlete.

Again, it is important to understand the coach's job. High school coaches help student-athletes train, stay motivated, improve skills, and give constructive feedback to players. Coaches of high school athletes often know about camps and showcases for student-athletes and can make recommendations on behalf of the student-athletes.

These coaches' primary jobs are not usually as coaches. High school coaches are often teachers and teaching is the job that pays most coaches' bills and supports their families. These men and women often teach five classes a day, monitor the cafeteria, halls, and sometimes parking lots, and often coach more than one sport. Coaches coach because they love the sport, the kids, and the competition – not because they are experts at marketing student-athletes. If a student-athlete asks a coach for assistance in the recruiting process, the student-athlete needs to realize that twenty other student-athletes also are asking the same coach for assistance. Even if coaches wanted to market student-athletes, coaches do not have the budgets or the time to send three profiles of each student-athlete to colleges, let alone the 100 profiles that are recommended to properly market even one student-athlete. Keep in mind, coaches may have relationships with certain college coaches, but, on average, a high school coach only has a relationship with three college coaches. Coaches do not have relationships or history with as many programs as a student-athlete needs to be exposed to in order to be marketed properly.

College coaches already know about Student-Athletes who get local media attention.

It is exciting for student-athletes and their parents when the media shows an interest in their abilities. In some towns, the local or even regional newspapers will run articles and large color photos of a particular student-athlete's accomplishments. Student-athletes who live in an area void of professional athletic teams will often be the focus of stories and interviews on local television and radio stations' sports segments. All of these things are good and fun and very complimentary to the student-athlete and his or her parents. After such media attention, student-athletes sometimes become almost mini "home-town heroes" and strangers recognize the student-athlete when he or she is out and about in that community. Due to this recognition factor, student-athletes and parents start to believe that *everyone* knows of and about this student-athlete and come to the false conclusion that college coaches also know of and about this student-athlete. Nothing can be farther from the truth.

College coaches do not discover talented student-athletes by reading newspaper articles with full color photos about them. A college coach in Iowa does not read any newspaper printed in the state of Nevada and vice versa. College coaches have no idea which student-athlete was on your evening television news station last night. Therefore, it is safe to say, college coaches do not know of or about your student-athlete even though it seems everyone within a 60-mile radius of where you live knows your student-athlete.

One more word about newspaper articles and media clips about or of student-athletes. When you contact a college coach, do not mail or email any articles about your student-athlete. No college coach is going to recruit or offer a scholarship to a student-athlete based on what a reporter has to say about the student-athlete's talent level, skill set, and ability. A reporter is not an expert in evaluating the talent and potential of a player in a particular sport, but the college coach is an expert in evaluating this. Sending newspaper clippings to a college coach is a waste of time and effort – these will be thrown away and never read. Keep such clippings for your scrapbooks at home.

Just because a student-athlete receives stacks of letters and mail from colleges does NOT mean the student-athlete is actually being recruited. Nor is it a true indication of a school's interest in that student-athlete.

It is vitally important to remember that mail is just that, mail. Colleges and universities send out a lot of mail to prospective students. College and university athletic programs send out a lot of mail to student-athletes. Names are gathered from various lists, and once a student-athlete's name is on some list, the student-athlete starts to get mail. Think of this as the athletic equivalent of normal junk mail. These pieces of mail are sent out indiscriminately to thousands of student-athletes. Often, the letter appears to be personally signed by the head coach. In reality, this is the work of a graduate or student assistant in that school's athletic department. The head coach does not know the student-athlete's name, nor does the head coach know the student-athlete was on the list to receive this piece of mail. This piece of mail is NOT any indication that a student-athlete is actually being recruited.

Often, this piece of mail will contain an invitation to an athletic camp at that school. Do not think this is a personal invitation to the camp or that, by going to the camp the student-athlete will necessarily get discovered or recruited. That camp invitation is merely an ad for the camp. Camps make extra money for coaches. The more student-athletes who attend a camp result in the more money the head coach can put into his or her personal income. This is not to say the camp will not be beneficial or worth while – quite the opposite. If a student-athlete displays exceptional skills at the camp, the student-athlete may draw the interest of the coaches at that college or university and be considered for recruitment afterward. In most cases, for the majority of student-athletes in attendance, the camp will be a great opportunity to improve skill sets and be coached by some very knowledgeable and experienced college coaches, but it is not where student-athletes get discovered or recruited. Most of the time, especially at the Division 1 level, the athletes who have an opportunity to be offered a scholarship by that coach are the athletes who were personally invited to the camp via phone or in person.

Also, in this piece of mail, a questionnaire may be included for a student-athlete to fill out and return to the school. ALWAYS complete that questionnaire and return it, even if the information has already been provided to that school in some other format (i.e. in an athletic resume or profile). Some one on the coaching staff will look over the returned and completed questionnaires and decisions will be made if the school should consider recruiting that particular student-athlete based on the answers on the questionnaire. Also, the questionnaire is a standardized form that the coaches at the particular school are familiar with. Coaches know where each and every piece of information is located on that questionnaire. If a coach wants to quickly know a student-athlete's GPA or ACT score, the coach knows exactly where to find the info on that form. If a coach only has a student-athlete's athletic resume, time may be wasted trying to locate particular information and a busy coach may decide not to bother with that student-athlete. When a questionnaire is received, the ideal way to handle it is to completely and neatly fill out the questionnaire, staple the student-athlete's profile or athletic resume to the back of it, and return it within five days.

College Recruiting Budgets

A word on college recruiting budgets: Not all budgets are equal. When most people think of college recruiting budgets, the perception is of universities having millions of dollars to spend each year on recruiting. While this is true for a few universities, this is not the norm. When all sports, schools, and recruiting budgets are factored in, the average coach has a recruiting budget of less than $500. Obviously, this small budget makes it very difficult to recruit nationally. Coaches must be very careful where and how money is spent. Most make certain no money in the recruiting budget is wasted. Coaches with small recruiting budgets are thrilled when a student-athlete that they wouldn't have known about makes the initial contact with them because it not only saves them time, but it also saves them money!

The following chart lists the top twenty NCAA D1/FBS recruiting budgets for the 2010-11 school year. The first thing to notice is the disparity between the men and women's recruiting budgets. Since Title IX, the numbers of female and male student-athletes on a campus are nearly the same, but the women's sport coaches must work with a drastically smaller budget (often for a greater number of sports teams if the school has a football program). The women's coaches recruit the same overall number of athletes with significantly less money. Consequently, it is vitally important that female student-athletes be proactive and market themselves to college coaches.

2010-11 NCAA D1/FBS Top 20 Recruiting Budgets

School	Conference	Total Recruitment Expenses	Men's Recruitment Expenses	Women's Recruitment Expenses
1. Tennessee	SEC	$2,296,023	$1,878,771	$417,252
2. Auburn	SEC	$2,117,645	$1,530,917	$586,728
3. Notre Dame	Big East	$2,070,316	$1,612,608	$457,708
4. Alabama	SEC	$1,694,202	$1,339,537	$354,665
5. Georgia	SEC	$1,540,743	$1,039,220	$501,523
6. Florida	SEC	$1,501,899	$1,065,716	$436,183
7. Georgia Tech	ACC	$1,489,599	$1,173,904	$315,695
8. Arkansas	SEC	$1,480,557	$1,060,500	$420,057
9. Michigan	Big Ten	$1,480,357	$1,039,948	$440,409
10. Texas	Big 12	$1,470,389	$989,370	$481,019
11. Marquette	Big East	$1,461,373	$1,289,560	$171,813
12. Kansas	Big 12	$1,454,154	$1,033,618	$420,536
13. North Carolina	ACC	$1,337,338	$949,396	$387,942
14. Illinois	Big Ten	$1,328,931	$962,345	$366,586
15. Duke	ACC	$1,313,378	$967,282	$346,096
16. Oklahoma	Big 12	$1,263,567	$837,890	$425,677
17. Kentucky	SEC	$1,260,065	$865,254	$394,811
18. Oregon	Pac-12	$1,235,968	$922,653	$313,315
19. Nebraska	Big Ten	$1,234,097	$888,165	$345,932
20. Texas Tech	Big 12	$1,184,799	$892,436	$292,363

The following chart shows the bottom ten NCAA D1/FBS recruiting budgets for the year 2010-11. (There are more than 100 NCAA D1/FBS schools, but the independents do not have to report their recruiting budgets nor do some schools in certain states such as Pennsylvania.) Notice that UAB's total recruiting budget is less than 18% of the University of Tennessee's total recruiting budget. Consequently, when the rosters of each school are examined, most student-athletes attending UAB are from the immediate area of Georgia and Alabama because the recruiting budget does not allow for air travel expenses for a great number of recruits. Conversely, the rosters of the University of Tennessee represent a national and international student-athlete population because the recruiting budget allows for extensive travel. This is one important factor for student-athletes and their parents to be aware of during the recruiting process. Just because a coach isn't flying a student-athlete to their campus or flying to make a home visit, does not indicate a lack of interest. In many cases, it is just an indication of a lack of funds. Also, schools with a smaller budget cannot afford to go searching for student-athletes who live at a distance from campus. Only if a coach is made aware of a student-athlete's existence, can a coach contemplate the best way to spend recruiting dollars on that athlete.

2010-11 NCAA D1/FBS Bottom 10 Recruiting Budgets

90. Wyoming	Mountain West	$474,568	$332,013	$142,555
91. Denver	Sun Belt	$451,405	$230,427	$220,978
92. SMU	Conference USA	$444,732	$290,043	$154,689
93. South Alabama	Sun Belt	$439,614	$308,886	$130,728
94. Ohio	MAC	$430,690	$296,483	$134,207
95. Tulane	Conference USA	$425,361	$305,021	$120,340
96. Florida International	Sun Belt	$420,873	$331,056	$89,817
97. Akron	MAC	$417,492	$267,595	$149,897
98. Buffalo	MAC	$414,567	$283,833	$130,734
99. New Mexico State	WAC	$411,905	$293,298	$118,607
100. UAB	Conference USA	$409,490	$234,669	$174,821

The following chart further breaks down the recruiting budgets of the University of Tennessee and Florida International University, both NCAA D1/FBS schools. Notice the difference in the recruiting budget of Tennessee's men's football and basketball teams. Football signs up to 25 recruits per year for a total of 85 scholarship players on a roster. Men's basketball typically signs three student-athletes per year and has a total of 13 scholarship student-athletes on a roster at one time. Tennessee's basketball budget is 11% of the football budget, which equals spending of approximately $50,000 to recruit student-athletes to fill one scholarship roster spot. The longer the recruiting process lasts and the longer the school has to spend money to recruit a player for one scholarship spot, the more money that is spent on that spot. This is one of the reasons college football programs plan to institute an early signing period for the sport of football.

Looking again at the University of Tennessee's recruiting budget, notice that the women's total recruiting budget is $417,252. For the sake of this example, assume that all ten women's sports split the recruiting money evenly (which is not the case, in actuality women's basketball would receive the greatest amount of recruiting dollars per spot). If divided evenly, each woman's sport would have a recruiting budget of $41,725. Taking Florida International's total recruiting budget and dividing it evenly across all nine women's sports, each team would have a recruiting budget of $9,979. It is obvious that Tennessee has much more to spend on recruiting nationally than FIU.

FIU had 56 female student-athletes on the track/cross country teams in the 2010-11 school year. Based on a five-year eligibility cycle, at least one fifth of the team (10 student-athletes) would be lost to graduation and need to be replaced. FIU would have had only $997.90 to recruit for each spot that the coach needed to fill. For the sake of this example, a gross underestimate of ten women (100 total) would need to be recruited to fill each of the ten spots. That would allow FIU to spend a maximum of $99.79 per student-athlete recruited. Clearly, less than $100 per recruit does not allow for air travel, hotel stays, and other costly recruiting tools available to a school with a larger budget like Tennessee. Once again, this illustrates how important it is to be proactive and place a student-athlete in front of the college coaches rather than waiting for a coach to discover a student-athlete.

School	Conference	Total Recruitment Expenses	Men's Recruitment Expenses	Women's Recruitment Expenses
1. Tennessee	SEC	$2,296,023	$1,878,771	$417,252

Tennessee's Football Recruiting Budget	$1,307,155
Tennessee's Men's Hoop Recruiting Budget	$150,000
$ Divided between 6 men's sports	$421,616
If evenly divided between 6 men's sports	
Amount per sport	$70,269
If divided evenly between 10 women's sports	
Amount per sport	$41,725

School	Conference	Total Recruitment Expenses	Men's Recruitment Expenses	Women's Recruitment Expenses
96. Florida International	Sun Belt	$420,873	$331,056	$89,817

If divided evenly between 9 women's sports	
Amount per sport	$9.979

* * *

The following chart is a list of the recruiting budgets for the year 2011 for D2 schools, all with football programs. Notice the difference between the lowest D1 budgets compared with the largest D2 budgets. The highest D2 recruiting budget is half of the lowest D1 recruiting budget. Coaches at the D2 level have a more difficult time recruiting than the D1 schools because many of the student-athletes are not familiar with or have never heard the name of the school prior to their recruitment. D2 coaches not only need to identify recruits and educate recruits about the school, but also have to try to fill their rosters on less than half the money. Obviously, when a student-athlete contacts a D2 coach, the coach is willing to take a good look at the student-athlete and is appreciative for the time and money that has been saved by that student-initiated contact.

2011 NCAA D2 Recruiting Budgets

Year	University	Men's Recruiting Expenses	Women's Recruiting Expenses
2011	Bemidji State University	$120,489	$86,116
2011	Minnesota State University-Mankato	$136,513	$60,669
2011	Saint Cloud State University	$115,751	$46,549
2011	Grand Valley State University	$110,820	$47,508
2011	Missouri Southern State University	$105,065	$49,806
2011	Northern State University	$84,155	$68,864
2011	Delta State University	$109,442	$40,588
2011	Northern Michigan University	$106,387	$35,033
2011	University of Minnesota-Duluth	$84,085	$54,195
2011	Michigan Tech University	$111,070	$26,686
2011	Minot State University	$65,492	$70,757
2011	Mercyhurst College	$78,474	$50,740
2011	Abilene Christian University	$81,423	$47,262

*All schools listed have a football program

Recruiting Services

Marketing, recruiting, and scouting companies that market student-athletes to colleges are numerous. These companies and agencies charge fees ranging from $500 to $4,000. In exchange, the company will help develop a profile for the student-athlete and email, fax, or mail it to any number of schools. Sometimes the fee also covers the cost of putting together a highlight film. The film and student athlete's profile are either sent to colleges in a mass distribution or are posted on the recruiting company's website. The problem is most of these companies do not do a very good job.

Recruiting companies usually send profiles to too few schools or send the profiles indiscriminately and impersonally to too many schools. When a bulk mailing arrives in a coaches' office either via email, fax, or the postal service, coaches do not appreciate having to take the time to sift through them. The coach knows that the student-athletes probably do not even know their profile has been sent to them so the student-athlete may not have any genuine interest in the school. To a coach, finding one recruit out of the hundreds of profiles sent is the equivalent of finding a needle in a haystack. A coach much prefers getting some personal contact directly from a student-athlete. The effort to contact the coach personally, rather than through a service, shows initiative and the willingness to work hard, which are things coaches admire in student-athletes.

Another problem with using a service is that some send out too many profiles to too many schools. There are numerous cases where a student-athlete is a legitimate D1 athlete but is flooded with offers from D2 and D3 schools because a profile was sent to all the schools in all the divisions indiscriminately. This results in much wasted time and efforts on the part of both the student-athlete and the college coaches.

Some sites post a student-athlete's profile and film to the company's website and expect college coaches to come to that website to look for recruits. In reality, most of those websites are unknown to coaches so the student-athlete is never even looked at by a college coach.

Before hiring such a company, it is important to understand what will be done, what won't be done, and how and when things will be done. Be certain to get all details in writing. Ask if they give any guarantees. Examine your heart and decide if where you attend college and participate in athletics is too important to leave up to someone else's whims. All the steps in the recruiting process can be done by a student-athlete and his or her parents, so why pay for someone else to do it?

Notes

Photo by Steve Fecht

"You miss 100 percent of the shots you never take."
Wayne Gretzky

Chapter 5

The Athletic Resume/Profile

The easiest way for most people to understand the recruiting process is to think of it like a job search. The student-athlete is trying to get a position on a team. Therefore, the student athlete needs to follow the same steps that one would use when job hunting. The **six simple steps** are:

1. Create a resume (aka athletic profile)
2. Write a cover letter
3. Research
4. Make initial contact
5. Follow up
6. Interview

How to Create a Profile

In order to introduce a student-athlete to college coaches and to let coaches know the student-athlete is interested in playing a sport at the next level, the student-athlete needs to create an athletic resume, also called a profile. All information on this profile must be accurate and as current as possible. This profile is valuable for a college program to determine whether or not there is interest in a student-athlete. Just like a resume for a job hunt, an athletic resume should fit completely on a single 8 ½ x 11 sheet of paper. The easiest way to create this athletic profile is in a computer spreadsheet file program like Microsoft Excel. To set it up, split the page into two columns (in half from left to right). Keep in mind there are numerous ways to create this athletic profile, this is not the only correct method of doing this, but this method is tried and proven to be successful.

Header

Centered, at the very top of the page, place the name of the student-athlete in bold print. Immediately under the name, add the student-athlete's graduation year. The reason the year must be in a prominent place is this – if a sophomore student-athlete sends a profile to a coach, and the coach likes everything on it and decides to pick up the phone and call the student-athlete, that coach would have to report a recruiting infraction to the NCAA. Generally, coaches aren't allowed to phone sophomores. No student-athlete wants to be the cause of the coach breaking NCAA rules.

The third line at the top of the athletic profile needs to indicate the position the student-athlete plays or the event in which the student-athlete participates. If, in a sport like football, the student-athlete plays multiple positions, list both or all. If, in a sport such a track and field or swimming, the student-athlete participates in many events, indicate the student-athlete's primary event at the top of the page and in the body of the athletic resume include times/measurements for all other events.

Adding a Photo

At the top left hand corner of the page, add a photo (a headshot) of the student-athlete. It is recommended that the photo be similar to a school yearbook picture in regular street attire. The purpose of this photo is so a coach can recognize this particular student-athlete when meeting them on campus. Many student-athletes believe it is best for this photo to be taken on team picture day so the student-athlete will be in uniform. Unfortunately, many photos taken on the team photo day are of the student-athlete's entire body, which is not useful for the purpose of this photo. Be certain the photo is a clear image of your face – no hats, helmets, etc.

Personal and Contact Info

The right side of the page is the place to put all of the student-athlete's personal and contact information. The very first lines need to include the student-athlete's mailing address, email address, home phone number, cell phone number, as well as a link or web address where the student-athlete's "highlights" may be viewed (if highlights are important for the sport). If it is appropriate for the student-athlete's sport, include the student-athlete's date of birth, height and weight. Also in this section, the student-athlete should list important college admissions type info such as GPA and ACT and SAT scores. If the ACT and/or SAT have not been taken but the student-athlete knows the date he or she will sit for one of these tests, it may be added in this spot.

Coaches' Contact Info

The following area on the right side of the page, separated by some space, is about the student-athlete's school and coach(es). List the name of the student-athlete's high school, the mailing address, main office phone number, as well as the student-athlete's counselor's name, phone number, and email address. Another line may be skipped for "white space" followed by the names of the student-athlete's coaches. Include each coach's title (ex. Head Coach, Club Coach, or Position/Event Coach) as well as the name of the school or club where the coach coaches. For each coach, list a phone contact as well as an email contact. In a perfect world, all coaches would love all student-athletes and, should a college coach contact the student-athlete's high school or club coach, only complimentary things would be said about the student-athlete. Unfortunately, we do not live in a perfect world. There are some situations where, for whatever reason, one coach does not think as highly of a student-athlete as another coach does. A student-athlete in this situation would want to list those coaches who will give a positive review of the student-athlete as a person as well as an athlete.

Athletic Stats

On the other side (left side) of the page, all of the student-athlete's pertinent stats are listed. If a student-athlete does not know what to include, the best person to ask is their coach. Football players will list some times as well as weight-lifting numbers. Swimmers and Track and Field athletes will list times and measurements in this spot. This is also the place to list the other positions played and any relevant information (times or measurements) regarding those positions.

Athletic Awards

Leave some space and then continue down the left side of the page adding a list of any awards or recognition the student-athlete has received in his or her sport career. Included in this section would be National/Regional/Sectional invitations, and All-City, All-League, All-State types of recognition. Be sure to also include any special awards received, even at the team level, such as "hardest worker", "Mr./Miss Hustle", and team captain to list a few. All of those awards give a college coach a better idea of the type of person the student-athlete is.

Academic Awards, Extracurricular Activities, Etc.

Again, leave some space and then list any extracurricular activities, student government positions, other sports played and the number of volunteer community service hours accumulated. College coaches like to see a student-athlete is well rounded and can juggle other activities while excelling in their sport. Other types of info that can be listed in this area can include the name of an employer and the number of hours worked per week, any AP credits received, as well as any academic honors received. If the student-athlete has a unique talent, list it here. If the student is fluent in a second language or has lived on an American Indian reservation or is a Native American, list that as well. The purpose of this is for the student-athlete to give the college coach the best idea of what this student-athlete is about and to make the student-athlete stand out in the college coach's mind.

When all of that information is compiled and inputted, print out a copy of the profile to make certain it prints out properly. The college coach will print the profiles of the student-athletes they choose to recruit. It is important that all of the columns and stats line up neatly and the entire profile prints on one single page.

On the following pages are three examples of excellent college profiles. Each of these student-athletes received D1 athletic scholarships.

MICHAEL JOSEPH
CLASS of 2007

04/08/2006

National Honor Society 2005, 2006
Academic All State Track and Field 2006
Academic Achievement Award 2004, 2005, 2006
Mathematics Department Award 2004, 2005, 2006
Social Studies Department Award 2005, 2006
Advanced Accounting Award 2006
Science Department Award 2006
Foreign Language Department Award 2005

ATHLETIC AWARDS:
Varsity Captain 2006
State Finals 2005, 2006
All State 2006
Regional Champion 2006
All Area 2005, 2006
All Area Dream Team 2005, 2006
All division 2005, 2006
Varsity Track Award 2004, 2005, 2006

POLEVAULT CAMPS
Jan Johnson, Chicago 2004, 2005, 2006
Turcheck Speed Camp 2006
University of MI Track and Field Camp 2005

ADDITIONAL INFORMATION:
03/00 - 03/03 - Lived in Göteborg, Sweden. Fluent in Swedish.
Attended International School of Göteborg Region, Grades 5-8

STUDENT DATA:

	Michael Joseph
	16981 A Drive
	North, MI 48100
Home Phone:	313.221.1234
Email Address:	mj@cc.net
Date of Birth:	10/10/89

ACADEMIC DATA:
Overall GPA:	4.0
ACT Test:	Taken 06/06
Comp Score	28
Writing Score	10/12
Desired Major:	Accounting/Law
NCAA:	Applied for Eligibility 07/06

ATHLETIC DATA:
Polevaulter
Height:	6'4"
Weight:	180

Track and Field Coach:
Bill C   109.234.5678
Vault Coach:
Mark Y   234.567.8901
Personal Record:
14'6" Summer Season 07/06
School Record 14'1" (Broke 1968 Record)

HIGH SCHOOL DATA:
Home Town High School
400 Main Street
North, MI 48100
Phone:	313.333.8820
Counselor:	Suzi Helpful
	313.333.8822

EXTRACURRICULAR:
President of Student Council 2006
National Honor Society
Weight Lifting w/Steve M
Speed Training w/Chris T
Pole Vault w/E. M. Training
Self Employed - Lawn Service

Kelsey Ebeth
Class of 2013
12205 First Lane
Knoxville, TN 37934
865-123-4567
swimgirl@gmail.com
D.O.B. 9/16/1994
Height: 5'10

Athletic Data and Stats:

Statistical Data
(Short Course Yards)

50 Free	25.2
100 Free	55.02
200 Free	02:07.8
500 Free	05:46.8
100 Breast	01:21.4
100 Fly	1:05
200 IM	2:24

Academic Data:

Overall GPA:	**4.0+**
Class Rank:	N/A
ACT Composite Score:	29 in April 2011
Desired Major:	Nursing

Hills and Valley High School
115 Valley Road
Knoxville, TN 37932
Academic Advisor:
Mary Helpful   865-678-1234
email: helpfumaryl@hillsandvalley.org

Academic Course Load includes

Honors Chemistry I & II, Honors Biology
Honors Spanish I & II, Honors English I, II
Honors Geometry, Honors Algebra II , Honors Pre-Calc
AP Chemistry, AP Government, AP English

Community Service: 100+ hours

Coach   Mike Michaels
Hills Recreation Association
City Aquatic Club
Coach.Michael@gmail.com
865-000-5678

Coach   Andy Andrews
Pool Aquatic Club
Hills and Valley High School
City Aquatic Club
coach.andrew@gmail.com
865-000-1234

Coach   Lizzie Flylady
Pool Aquatic Club   (PACK)
flylady@poolaquaticclub.com
865-000-6789

Athletic Awards:

CHRA	Hardest Worker 2009-2011
PACK	Hardest Worker Junior Group 2010
HVA	State Qualifier 2010-2011
	All City Meet Finalist 2010-2011
GKAISA	City Meet Finalist 2007-2011

Made Southeastern cuts in 50 & 100 Free 2011
Made Senior Sectional Cut in 50 Free 2011

Work Experience:
Assisted in coaching summer league teams 06-:
Lifeguard: Country Club 2010-2011

	Green Pool	2010
	The Hills Pool	2010-2011

JOSEPH MATTHEWS
CLASS OF 2014
OL/DT

STUDENT DATA:

Joseph Matthews
1830 Valencia Dr.
El Paso, TX 79925

Home Phone:	915.465.1199
Email Address:	joematt@comcast.net
Date of Birth:	1/30/95

ATHLETIC DATA:

Height:	6'5"
Weight:	260
Bench:	320
Squat:	475
Clean:	305
Vertical Jump:	29"
Position:	OL/DT
Coach:	Clint Zander, Football
	913-222-3456
	ZanderC@gmail.com
Coach:	Steve Theman, Strength
	202-334-8800
	Theman@aol.com

EXTRACURRICULAR:

Fellowship of Christian Athletes (FCA)
Students Against Destructive Decisions (SADD)
President, Student Council

ACADEMIC DATA:

Overall GPA:	3.6
ACT:	28
Desired Major:	Pre-Med

ATHLETIC AWARDS:

Varsity Captain
All State
All Area
First Team Metro West
All Conference (OT)
All State Academic - Football
State/National Record Holder with NAP
(Nat'l Alliance of Powerlifters) Bench & Clean

HIGH SCHOOL DATA:

Jefferson High School
457 Center Road
El Paso, TX 79925

Phone:	915-230-2000
Counselor:	Tim Templeton
	915-230-2001
	Ttemp@Jefferson.org

Football Camps

National Underclassmen Combine
Football University
Scout.com Showcase
US Army All American Combine

ACADMIC AWARDS

All State Academic
National Honor Society
Academic Acheivement Award

Photo by Steve Fecht

"Success isn't a result of spontaneous combustion. You must set yourself on fire."

Arnold H. Glasgow

Chapter 6

Writing a Cover Letter

The second step in the recruiting process is to write a letter of introduction, or a cover letter. The cover letter will be sent with the student-athlete's profile to college coaches at all the schools that are of interest to the student-athlete. (Dream schools, even if the student-athlete believes there is no chance of playing at that school, should not be eliminated.) If schools are not contacted, the student-athlete has no chance of playing for those schools. Ideally, this should be done the summer before the student-athlete's junior year, or at the completion of the student-athlete's first varsity season.

The cover letter should be short and to the point. No college coach has time to read a lengthy letter – they prefer to see lots of "white space" on the piece of paper. Each letter is sent, usually via email but the U.S. Postal Service may be used as well. The letter needs to be addressed to a specific coach by name. The student-athlete will have to do some research on the Internet to find the names of the head coaches and others coaches at colleges and universities. There are tips for finding this information quickly and easily under the "Research" heading of this book.

Salutation/Greeting

In the cover letter, the student-athlete will introduce him or herself and list their graduation year, position, and high school. The letter will be sent to a specific coach and that coach's name will be included in the salutation. Student-athletes need to prepare letters for as many coaches as necessary at each school. For instance, if you play on the defensive line in football, you would send a letter to the head coach, defensive coordinator, the defensive line coach, the recruiting coordinator, a grad assistant who works in recruiting, and possibly the director of football operations. The more eyes that see a student-athlete's letter and profile, the more chances that student-athlete has of having someone see something positive about the student-athlete. Even though the student-athlete is sending the cover letter with the profile to six different coaches, this would still be considered one contact because it is only one school.

Body of Letter

In the body of the letter, the student-athlete must concisely state an interest in participating in collage athletics at that school, and, if possible, an interest in a major or program of study. Also, the fact that the student-athlete's profile is being sent as an attachment is important to mention. If the student-athlete has "highlights" that are viewable on the Internet, be sure to include the link to those highlights in the letter. The link may also be included on the student-athlete's profile.

Closing

The closing line of the letter should be "Go Bears" or whatever the actual team nickname is at that particular school. Under the student-athlete's signature, contact info for the student-athlete needs to be listed.

*Please see sample cover letter on the following page

Sample Cover Letter to Coach

Dear Coach Jones,

My name is Morgan Jones and I am a point guard at Jefferson High School in Sarasota, FL. I am in the Class of 2016. I wish to compete athletically in college while earning a degree in Engineering. Virginia Tech has a great reputation both academically and athletically and I believe would be a perfect fit for me.

I am attaching my athletic resume. Please look it over and let me know if you will have a spot on your roster for me in the fall of 2016.

If you require any more info, please don't hesitate to contact me.

Go Hokies!
Sincerely,
Morgan Jones
Cell Phone: 941-221-1233
Home Phone: 941-886-6778
Email: MorganJones@gmail.com

Highlights may be viewed at: www.youtube.morganjones.com

Photo by Steve Fecht

**"Whether you think you can or whether you think you can't,
you're right!"**

Henry Ford

Chapter 7

Research Who to Contact

The next step in the recruiting process is doing some research. Student-athletes must decide which schools to send profiles and cover letters to. It is important to find the schools that typically roster players that are of like size, style, speed, skill set, and ability as the student-athlete. (Do research on the Internet to find these schools. Also, ask high school coaches for suggestions.) Keep in mind; the student-athlete must be a fit for schools academically as well as athletically.

Marketing a student-athlete is really not much different than marketing any other product. The more exposure a product/student-athlete has, the greater the chances of success for the product/student-athlete. As with products, the market is not randomly flooded. Rather, a product launch is researched and well planned. The product is introduced and marketed in areas where the potential for success is high. Student-athletes and their parents need to research which schools are likely to be interested in the student-athlete. If a student-athlete is an average to better than average player, some coach somewhere would love to have that student-athlete on his or her roster. The tough job is finding that coach and marketing the student-athlete to that coach.

Other Topics to Research

Is there a need at the student-athlete's position?
If the student-athlete is a 100 freestyle swimmer and a school has five swimmers on the roster who compete in that event (one per class), that school is probably not looking for another 100 freestyle swimmer. Look over the

rosters of schools to see how many student-athletes are rostered per position and decide whether or not there is a need for another. Take into consideration how many seniors will be leaving due to graduation.

How many scholarships are available at the school?

While it is difficult to know exactly how many scholarships are in use per sport at every school, it is easy to learn what the maximum number of scholarships that are allowed per sport/team, per division within a college athletic governing body. Once a student-athlete gets farther along in the recruiting process and beings talking directly to college coaches, this is a question that should be asked of the coach.

Does the school have your major?

Not every school has every major. If a student-athlete has their heart set on a particular major, it is important to know whether or not it is offered at the school.

What are the stats of the athlete's on the school's current roster?

Check out the heights and weights of the current athletes on the school's roster at the student-athlete's position. Is the student-athlete of similar size or within the range of sizes listed? What are the times/measurements of the student-athlete's on the roster in the past year or two of competition? Does the student-athlete compare to those athletes? If only a small distance or amount of time exists between the athlete's on the present roster and the student-athlete, the school may be interested in the student-athlete.

Which Schools to Contact

When researching schools, do not forget that the NCAA is not the only governing body in college athletics. Please refer to Chapter 3 of this book and read the information on the other governing organizations. There are over 2270 institutions where student-athletes can play at the next level. Here is a quick recap of the governing bodies:

College Athletic Governing Bodies

NCAA, ncaa.org (346 D1 members, 291 D2, and 439 D3)

NAIA naia.org (300 members in D1 and D2)

NJCAA njcaa.org (525 members)

NCCAA thenccaa.org (111 members in D1 and D2)

USCAA uscaa.org (80+ members in D1 and D2 with 500 to 2500 students per school)

CCAA ccaa.ca (100 members)

CIA www.cis-sic.ca (56 members)

For your information, the next few pages contain listings of the maximum number of scholarships awarded by NCAA D1 and D2 schools as well as the NAIA, NJCAA, and NCCAA schools. (For more information, refer to Chapter 3 of this guide.)

NCAA DIVISION I MEN'S VARSITY SPORTS

Scholarship limit per Member School	NCAA I
Baseball	11.7
Basketball - NCAA I is a head count sport*	13
Fencing	12.6
Football - NCAA FBS	85
Football - NCAA FCS	63
Golf	4.5
Gymnastics	6.3
Ice Hockey	18
Lacrosse	12.6
Skiing	3.6
Soccer	6.3
Swimming & Diving	9.9
Tennis	4.5
Track & Field/Cross Country	12.6
Volleyball	4.5
Water Polo	4.5
Wrestling	9.9

* A head count sport means full scholarships cannot be split between athletes

WOMEN'S VARSITY SPORTS

Scholarship limit per Member School	NCAA I
Basketball - NCAA I is a head count sport*	15
Field Hockey	12
Golf	6
Gymnastics - NCAA I is a head count sport*	12
Ice Hockey	18
Lacrosse	12
Rowing	20
Soccer	12
Softball	12
Swimming & Diving	8.1
Tennis - NCAA I is a head count sport*	8
Track & Field /Cross Country	18
Volleyball - NCAA I is a head count sport*	12

* A head count sport means full scholarships cannot be split between athletes

NCAA Division 2 Scholarship Limits per Member School

Sport	Men	Women
Baseball	9.0	-
Basketball	10.0	10.0
Bowling	-	**5.0**
Cross-country/track & field	**12.6**	12.6
Equestrian	-	**15.0**
Fencing	**4.5**	4.5
Field hockey	-	6.3
Football	36.0	-
Golf	3.6	5.4
Gymnastics	5.4	6.0
Ice hockey	13.5	**18.0**
Lacrosse	10.8	9.9
Rifle	**3.6**	-
Rowing	-	**20.0**
Rugby	-	**12.0**
Sand volleyball	-	**5.0**
Skiing	**6.3**	6.3
Soccer	9.0	9.9
Softball	-	7.2
Swimming and diving	8.1	8.1
Tennis	**4.5**	6.0
Volleyball	**4.5**	8.0
Water polo	**4.5**	**8.0**
Wrestling	9.0	-

NAIA – Number of Scholarships Per School Per Sport

- Baseball = 12
- Basketball D1 = 11
- Basketball D2 = 6
- Cross Country = 5
- Football = 24
- Golf = 5
- Soccer = 12
- Softball = 10
- Swimming & Diving = 8
- Tennis = 5
- Track & Field = 12
- Wrestling = 8
- Volleyball = 8

NJCAA Maximum Number of Scholarships Per School Per Sport

MEN	WOMEN
Baseball – 24	Basketball – 16
Basketball – 16	Golf – 8
Football – 85	Ice Hockey – 16
Golf – 8	Lacrosse – 20
Ice Hockey – 16	Soccer – 18
Lacrosse – 20	Softball – 24
Soccer – 18	Tennis – 8
Tennis – 8	Track & C.C. – 30
Track & C.C. – 30	Volleyball – 14
Water Polo – 4.5	Water Polo – 8
Wrestling – 16	

Easy Ways to Find Contact Information

One of the best ways to find which sports teams are on campus at NCAA schools, is to use the NCAA website. There is a quick and easy way to navigate the website to find this information:

1. Go to: www.eligibilitycenter.com, click on "ENTER HERE"
2. On the top menu bar, click "Sports"
3. Click the red arrow at the bottom of the text
4. A list of sports will appear, organized by season – click the sport of interest
5. A menu appears listing the three divisions – click the one of interest
6. An entire list will appear with every school with that sport at that division
7. Clicking on any school will take you directly to that school's website

Once on the school's athletic website, find the "directory" or "staff directory" listing. This is a list of the name of every employee in the athletic department as well as their title/position, their phone numbers and email addresses. Scroll down the list to find the sport of interest and use this information to build a contact list. Profiles and cover letters should be sent to all of the contacts you accumulate. It is helpful to have a separate list so you can easily refer back to it later in the process when you wish to follow up.

Another quick and easy way to find this information is to do an Internet search for "List of NCAA Schools and Conferences by Sport" or "List of NCAA Schools and Conferences by Division".

To find contact information for schools and coach in the NCCAA, use their membership directory at: http://www.thenccaa.org/custompages/2013-14%20Membership%20Directory.pdf

College Scouting Form

Name of University/College: _____

Freshman Year Academics

Average High School GPA: _____

Average Class Rank: _____

Average SAT/ ACT Scores: _____

Freshman Admission Requirements

High School Diploma/ GED Requirements: _____

The number of academic requirements: _____

GPA requirements: _____

SAT/ ACT requirements: _____

Costs

Tuition: _____

Room and Board: _____

Books: _____

Other Fees: _____

Financial Aid

Types of Aid: _____

Required Forms: _____

Deadlines: _____

Academics

Majors: _____

Academic Requirements: _____

Class Size: _____

School Enrollment: _____

Athletics: _____

Activities: _____

Diversity: _____

Setting: Rural   Urban   Suburban

Distance From Home: _____

Photo by R. Grant

"To uncover your true potential you must first find your own limits. Then you have to have the courage to blow past them."

Picabo Street

Chapter 8

Make Contact

One of the biggest mistakes student-athletes make in the recruiting process is not contacting enough schools. Ideally, a student-athlete should be marketed to 100 to 300 colleges and universities. The minimum number of contacts is 75 with profiles and letters going to schools in all divisions, especially if the student-athlete is uncertain at which level they will be able to compete. This is not to suggest that a mass mailing of a form letter be sent to 300 schools (which is exactly what some of the 'for fee' services do). Marketing a student-athlete to colleges requires communicating with each school individually. This requires research and organization.

Keep in mind that the response a student-athlete can expect to receive from colleges will be approximately 10%. This is another reason it is vitally important to make plenty of contacts.

Parent Traps

Parents often create roadblocks for student-athletes during this phase of the process. Moms are guilty of drawing a circle on a map that equates to a three hour driving radius from home and limiting the student-athlete to schools only in that circle. It is a fact that a student-athlete may be more valuable to an out-of-state school than to an in-state school. Colleges and universities all want to be as diverse as possible and one way to show diversity is to have students from each of the 50 states.

Dads tend to be guilty of playing the "name game". If the student-athlete gets a piece of mail from, what the dad considers to be, a "big name" school, all other schools become irrelevant to him. Be careful not to eliminate any schools.

Diversity

College athletic programs like to be diverse as well. To prove this point, look at the map below. This was taken directly out of the University of Tennessee 2009 football media guide. The map shows that players on their football team are from 19 states as well as the District of Columbia. Clearly, if a school is boasting about this to the media, it is of great worth!

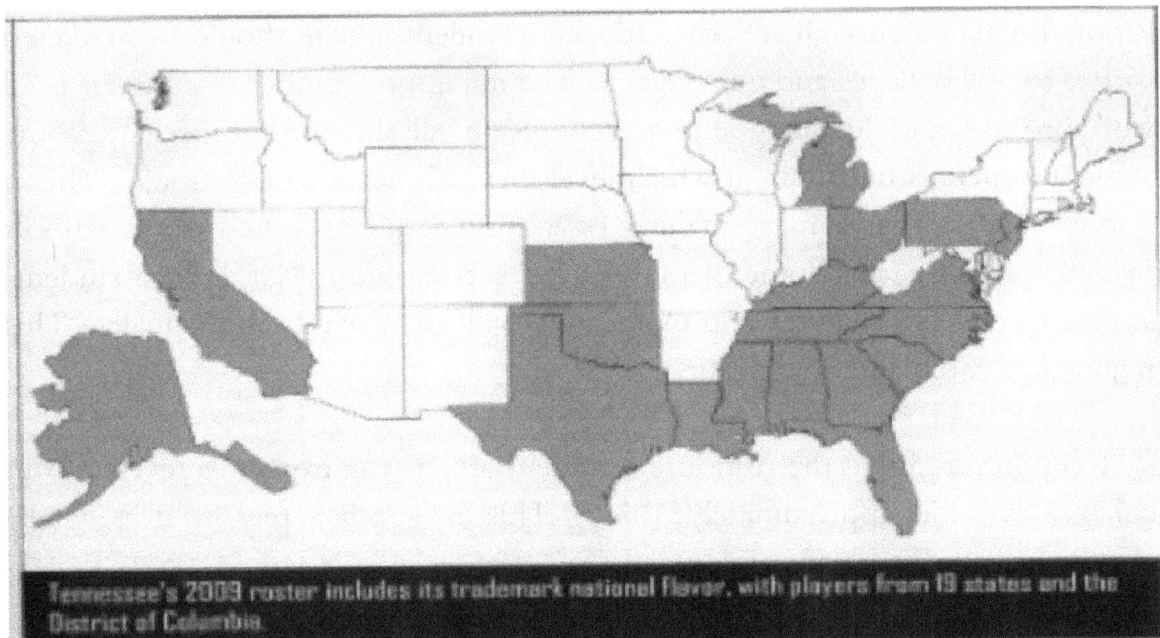

Tennessee's 2009 roster includes its trademark national flavor, with players from 19 states and the District of Columbia.

Notes

Photo by Steve Fecht

**"The more difficult the victory, the greater the happiness
in winning."**

Pele

Chapter 9

Follow Up

If there is a particular school that a student-athlete is interested in, the student-athlete should never hesitate to pick up the telephone and call the position coach or recruiting coach at that school. Many high school students do not have the poise or confidence to place a personal phone call to a college coach. Yet, a phone call from a prospective recruit will get the coach's attention and make a student-athlete much more memorable to the coach. After all, if a coach is going to recruit a student-athlete, the coach is going to be developing at least a four-year relationship with the athlete. The sooner the relationship begins the better.

On the other hand, as much as a coach is impressed with a polite phone call from a student-athlete, a coach can potentially be turned off to a student-athlete if the student-athlete's parents phone the coach. Coaches do not coach parents. A meddling parent can be a thorn in a coach's side and can hurt a student-athlete's chances of being recruited by some schools. This is not to suggest that parents should not be actively involved in the marketing and recruiting process. Parents should be involved with and should be supportive of their student-athletes at this important time in their lives.

Think of the recruiting process as "dating." How involved is a parent in the dating process? Certainly, parents want to meet the person their son or daughter is dating. It helps parents like the person their son or daughter is dating. But, if the person their son or daughter is dating is completely unacceptable, does not share the same values as the son or daughter, or is in some other way objectionable, then the parent has an obligation and a right to voice that opinion to their son or daughter. Does a parent pick up the telephone to tell their son or daughter's friend how much the son or daughter likes them and wants to spend time with them? Probably not -- so a parent should not pick up the phone to chat with a coach either. As with dating, if a coach is interested in a student-athlete and the student-athlete happens to phone the coach, the coach is flattered that the interest is mutual.

Keep Organized

A file box should be created to keep every communication with college coaches in an organized manner. Manila folders should be used inside the file box. As the student-athlete begins to receive mail from coaches, write the name of the school on the file tab and place it alphabetically in the file box. This folder will become a communications log. Every piece of information received from a college needs to be kept in the folder marked with that college's name, as does a list of every item sent to the school by the student-athlete. The name, address, and telephone number of the coach, and academic program of interest should be noted in this folder as well. The file box should be kept in the same location during the recruiting process so the student-athlete can easily access it during phone conversations with college coaches. If further interest develops in this school, having all the information in one easily accessible place will pay dividends.

Once the file box is set up with folders for schools, it is easy to communicate with any coach from any school that may contact the student-athlete. Every conversation or communication with anyone at that particular school will be noted in the folder. It is important to write a summary of every conversation (write these directly on the inside of the folder itself) including the name and title of the person with which the student-athlete spoke, the time, date, and method of communication (email, telephone conversation, etc.). If anything is requested from the student-athlete (ex. an application), the folder should be flagged with a sticky note until the request is fulfilled. In the event of an unexpected phone call from any school, a quick glance at the folder will refresh the student-athlete's memory and allow the student-athlete to get necessary information and be more conversational.

Take Notes

Any time the student-athlete will be talking with college coaches in person or on the phone, the student-athlete needs to look over the folder prior to the conversation. It is important to review previous conversations. It is also important, if a coach mentions in those conversations something about his personal life, to make note of it. For example, if in a previous phone conversation the coach mentioned it was his son's birthday and the family was having a small celebration, the next time the student-athlete talks to that coach, the student-athlete should inquire about the birthday party. This impresses the coach because the student-athlete has remembered something that is important to the coach. Coaches know the importance of taking notes when they speak to recruits – they do it regularly and refer to them prior to making phone calls to student-athletes. Student-athletes need to use this same technique. It is very effective.

Calling College Coaches

Since student-athletes will only hear back from 10% of the schools they contact, it is important that contact is made with the schools where the student-athlete really has an interest. Student athletes can always call college coaches but college coaches may only call student-athletes according to the NCAA rules of contact. Therefore, if a student-athlete phones a college coach and that coach does not return the call, the student-athlete should not be discouraged. It may be a "dead period" or some other period when coaches cannot call student-athletes and the coach did not return the call because it would be an NCAA violation.

When calling a college coach, the student-athlete should ask if the coach received the student-athlete's letter and profile. In football, it is best to call the position coach or recruiting coordinator rather than the head coach.

If At First You Don't Succeed, Re-Evaluate and Re-Send

If, after sending out profiles and cover letters, the student-athlete gets a return interest from fewer than 10% of the schools contacted, the game plan should be adjusted. Perhaps the student-athlete contacted too few schools and more cover letters and profiles should be sent out. Perhaps the student-athlete has targeted the wrong division of schools to contact. If a student-athlete is not a prospective recruit at a school, most coaches will not bother to let the student athlete know this. If there appears to be less interest in the student-athlete than hoped for, the student-athlete may want to target one division lower or perhaps even contact schools that are under the umbrella of a different governing body.

Ask the Tough Questions

When the student-athlete does speak with a college coach, it is important to ask questions that may feel awkward to the student-athlete. The first question should be if the student-athlete would be a "fit" for that coach's program. If the coach indicates that the student-athlete is NOT a fit, the student-athlete should ask the reason. In this situation, the student-athlete needs to be gracious and move on. It is important that the student-athlete is courteous and polite at all times. The college coaching world is very small and all the coaches know one another. Often, coaches run into each other in airports and other various places and it is not unusual for one coach to ask another if there are any athletes that their school is unable to recruit, for whatever reason, that may be a fit at the other coach's school. Student-athletes want coaches to pass their name along to other coaches. This is a high compliment and coaches give those recommendations much weight and consider those to be most credible.

Moving On – Do Not Focus On Rejection

It is vitally important that the student-athlete NOT take rejection personally. Again, there are many reasons for rejection. Perhaps the school has too many athletes at the student-athlete's position. Maybe the school has reached the scholarship limit. The student-athlete needs to move on from rejection and think in terms of the NEXT school on the list.

Recruiting Boards

There is a scene in the movie "We Are Marshall" which shows the head coach with the "recruiting board". There are many columns on the board, headed by the titles of one of the positions of need. Under the title, there is a list of names. The coach talks to each of the prospective student-athletes in the order the names appear on the board. As each is rejected, the coach crosses the name of the athlete off the list and moves on to the next one. The attitude of

"NEXT" is the mentality the student-athlete needs to develop during this process.

It cannot be stressed enough that the student-athlete needs to be in conversations with as many schools as possible. The more schools that are interested means more potential to play at the next level.

Questions to Ask a College Coach

- How many student-athletes are you recruiting at my position?
- What position will I play on your team?
- Will I be red-shirted my first year?
- Where am I on your recruiting depth chart?
- How many student-athletes play my position on your current roster?
- Realistically, where will I fit into your program? As a role player? As a practice squad player? As a starter?
- When can I anticipate being a regular player or starter on the team?
- If financial aid is offered, what happens if I get injured? Become academically ineligible? Take classes summer term? What is the likelihood that this financial aid package will be renewed, increased, or decreased over the course of my college career?
- Must I attend a tryout to be on the team or am I guaranteed a spot on the roster?
- What expectations do you have for conditioning and training?
- What is your coaching style? (Does this style match my learning style?)
- When does the coach's contract expire? How long does the coach intend to stay? How long has the coach been at this school? What about the coaches at my position? If the head coach leaves the school, what happens to my athletic scholarship?
- If I am seriously injured while competing, who is responsible for my medical expenses?
- What happens if I don't like your school and wish to transfer?
- What is a typical day for a student athlete?
- How many credits do your athletes carry per term?
- Is academic assistance available to your student-athletes?
- What percentage of players on athletic scholarship graduate?
- What is the team G.P.A.?
- Does my athletic scholarship cover tuition, fees, room, board, and books? What exactly will and will not be covered by my athletic scholarship?
- If I do not complete my degree within four years, is there any additional scholarship money available?

"Show me an athlete who is afraid to look bad, and I'll show you an athlete you can beat every time."

Lou Brock

Chapter 10

The Interview/The Visit

There are two types of campus visits -- official visits and unofficial visits. It is very easy to differentiate between the two types of visits. Official visits occur during the student-athletes senior year of high school and are paid for by the college; unofficial visits can be made prior to the senior year of high school and are paid for by student-athlete and/or the student-athlete's parents.

Unofficial Visits

Any visit to a college campus that is self-funded by a prospective student-athlete and a student-athlete's parents is considered an unofficial visit. Unofficial visits can be made at any time, even prior to the senior year of high school. When on an unofficial visit, the school may provide the student-athlete with complimentary tickets to a home athletics contest. A student-athlete and a student-athlete's parents may make an unofficial visit at any time, and the number of unofficial visits that may be made by a student-athlete is unlimited. If a student-athlete makes an unofficial visit to a campus during a "Dead Time," coaches are not permitted to talk with the student-athlete or the student-athlete's parents.

If a student-athlete is invited on an unofficial visit by a coach, the student-athlete usually will have an opportunity to meet the coaches while on campus. Often an unofficial visit includes a visit to the sidelines prior to a sporting event. Sometimes a campus tour is arranged for the student-athlete – transportation around campus may be provided on an unofficial visit. To take full advantage of the time on campus, student-athletes may opt to schedule appointments with the school's admissions representatives, financial aid coordinators, and representatives from the various college departments.

Unofficial visits can be used as an opportunity to check out the school. While on campus, eat a meal in the dining hall, walk through buildings while classes are in session, pick up a copy of the campus newspaper, and ask athletes for their opinions about the school. It is important that student-athletes and anyone accompanying the student-athlete on the visit take notes while on campus. After a number of college visits, the student-athlete may experience information overload, making it difficult to differentiate between schools. (Please see the "College Evaluation Sheet" on page 87.)

If a student-athlete hopes to meet and talk with the coach while on campus, it is important to make certain that the visit is not during a "dead period." It is best to phone or email the coach prior to planning any visit if the student-athlete wants to meet with him or her.

Weekends and holidays are often the easiest times for families to get to college campuses, but these are not the ideal times to visit. If possible, try to visit college campuses during the week when classes are in session. It is difficult to get a feel for a college community if the students are not present.

Official Visits

During the senior year of high school, a student-athlete may be invited to visit a college campus on an Official Visit. On this type of visit, the school pays for some or all of the visiting student-athlete's expenses. Covered expenses may include transportation, lodging, and meals. If a student-athlete is invited on an Official Visit, it is an indication that the student-athlete is being seriously considered for an athletic scholarship from the school.

Student-athletes are limited to a total of five Official Visits. These visits may be divided between Division I and Division II schools. Official Visits made to a Division III school does not count in the five-visit limit. It is important for student-athletes to make wise choices when accepting Official Visits. It may be more advantageous to make an Unofficial Visit to a school within driving distance and to save Official Visits for visits requiring an overnight stay. If a student-athlete plays more than one sport, it is important to know that the total Official Visits allowed is five, not five visits per sport. In other words, if a student-athlete accepts three Official Visits to check out

Volleyball programs, and two Official Visits to check out Basketball programs, the student-athlete will have used his or her five visits.

An Official Visit must take place after the first day of classes of a student-athlete's senior year. Prior to an Official Visit, the college must have a copy of the invited student-athlete's high school transcript and standardized test scores from the ACT, SAT, PSAT, or PLAN. Official Visits may last only 48 hours in duration starting from the time the student-athlete arrives on campus. If a coach accompanies or transports a student-athlete to campus for an Official Visit, the 48-hour clock begins ticking the moment the trip begins.

Meals and lodging for a student-athlete's parents, legal guardians, or spouse may be paid for by the school on an Official Visit, but expenses for siblings and friends may not be paid for by the school. Transportation costs for the student-athlete may be paid for by the school but not for the student-athlete's parent. If a student-athlete and his or her parent travel to the school by car, gas money may be paid as long as the reimbursement is made to the student-athlete and not the parent. If a student-athlete travels with a coach or friend to the school in a vehicle not owned by the student-athlete or the student-athlete's immediate family, gas mileage may not be paid.

Parents

Parents should always be welcome on Official Visits. If a coach discourages a student-athlete from bringing a parent on an Official Visit, be sure to find out the reasoning behind the recommendation. Choosing where a student-athlete will spend the next four or five years of life is a daunting task so the more eyes, ears, and evaluations available to a student-athlete usually leads to a better decision. Sometimes it is not possible for a parent to accompany a student-athlete on an Official Visit. When this is the case, the student-athlete and his or her parents should prepare a comprehensive list of questions and places to see before the student-athlete's visit. Bringing a camera and taking many photos is a great way to document a visit if a student-athlete must travel alone to a school.

Student-Athletes are Always Being Evaluated

During an Official Visit, the student-athlete must remember they are being evaluated the minute they arrive on campus. The coach has eyes and ears everywhere. It is not unheard of for a secretary or janitor to report information back to a college coach. It is imperative the student-athlete is on his or her best behavior the moment the visit begins.

Hosts

When visiting a school on an Official Visit is customary for the student-athlete to be assigned to a student host. The student host is usually a non-senior member of the team – a potential teammate if the student-athlete chooses to attend that school. The host's responsibilities are to answer questions, guide the student-athlete around campus, and entertain the student-athlete. An entertainment stipend of not more than $30 is provided to the host for this purpose. The NCAA has strict regulations about how this money is spent and any violation can cause the school and the prospective student-athlete to lose NCAA eligibility. The money may be used to pay for costs associated with entertainment, such as snacks, food, movies, admissions, etc. The money may NOT be used to purchase souvenirs or any article of clothing such as hats, t-shirts, sweatshirts, etc.

When on an Official Visit, coaches often prefer the student-athlete stay in the dorm with the student host. This is an excellent opportunity for the student-athlete to experience what life on campus is like. Often the student-host will reside with or near other members of the team, which gives the student-athlete a better idea whether or not he or she is comfortable in the environment and compatible with the other members of the team. Keep in mind the student host's job is to entice the student-athlete to attend that school, so the student host may not be as forthright as other students when answering questions.

The host usually makes a great impression and often student-athletes feel they can relax and "let their guard down" with the host. This is a major mistake. Student-athletes need to think of the host as a SPY - a spy for the coach. After the visit, the host will be called into the coach's office and will share his or her impressions of the student-athlete. The host will report anything that is said or done that may not be desirable to the coach and the school's program. This is the reason the student-athlete must be on his or her best behavior with the host. The student host may appear to be the student-athlete's best friend, but the student host's loyalty is to the coach, not the visiting student-athlete. Everything a student-athlete says and does while in the company of the student host may be reported back to the coaching staff.

More Rules and Regulations

Over the years, there have been many violations of NCAA regulations regarding Official Visits. Due to some highly publicized gross violations, the NCAA now requires schools to inform student-athletes prior to an Official Visit that sex, drugs, and gambling will not be part of the visit. Before embarking on an Official Visit, it is recommended that the student-athlete review the rules and regulations of Official Visits, which may be found on the NCAA's website.

Colleges Can't Invite Everyone on Official Visits

Division I sports are limited in the number of Official Visits offered to student-athletes each year. Football is allowed 56 Official Visits, basketball 12, and baseball 25. Obviously, only the most coveted student-athletes are invited on Official Visits.

Meeting/Talking With a College Coach

College coaches like to interact with student-athletes who treat them as a priority, even if they are not. Student-athletes need to use basic manners and engage in common courtesies when speaking to college coaches.

Dress to Impress the Coach

The student-athlete does not need to dress up to meet a coach, but clean and neat clothes are required. The student-athlete should consider any meeting with a college coach as a business meeting and the student-athlete should dress accordingly. One general rule, clothing must be free from rips, stains, holes, and wrinkles.

Clothing chosen should compliment and emphasize the student-athlete's physique. For example, if the student athlete has well-developed neck muscles, it would not be wise for that student-athlete to wear a turtleneck. If a student-athlete has skinny, under-developed calf muscles, the student-athlete should not wear a skirt. If a student-athlete has sculpted biceps and triceps, the student-athlete should consider a shirt with short sleeves. Always try to accentuate the student-athlete's best physical features. Remember: The student-athlete is the product and the goal is to motivate the coach to buy the product (extend an offer to the student-athlete to play college athletics at the coach's school).

Male Student-Athletes

The male student-athlete should wear neat and clean jeans, shorts, or khaki pants. If a student-athlete wears jeans, the jeans should be worn with a belt, in other words, no sagging. Some sort of collared shirt is most appropriate. A button-front shirt can be worn open over a t-shirt or a polo style shirt may be worn. Athletic shoes are acceptable.

Female Student-Athletes

Female student-athletes should wear a modest skirt or pants with a modest top (no bare midriffs). Jewelry, make-up, and hairstyle should compliment the outfit and not be distracting to either the coach or the student-athlete. Student-athletes, who cannot walk easily and comfortably in high heels, should not wear them. (The coach should remember the student-athlete for her athleticism, not for falling off her platform stilettos.)

Manners

Coaches are impressed with student-athletes who are polite and exhibit good manners. When meeting and greeting a coach, student-athletes should arrive early or at least be on time. Student-athletes need to smile and extend their right hand for a handshake. Eye contact should be made and maintained with the coach as the student-athlete and the coach exchange greetings. The student-athlete must verbally thank the coach for the opportunity to meet with the coach, visit the campus, and whatever else might be appropriate at that time.

Thank You Note

After all interactions with college coaches, it is a good idea to follow up the visit/meeting with a personally signed thank you note. This note should be mailed to the coach no more than 48 hours after the meeting. An email is not as good but it is acceptable. Manners, and the lack of, will make a student-athlete memorable to college coaches. It is important for student-athletes to be remembered by coaches in a positive way. Coaches want to sign student-athletes who will reflect well on the coach, the team, and the university in a positive way.

Have Rehearsed Responses Ready

No coach wants student-athletes to be distracted from their sports and their studies. Coaches want student-athletes who have definite goals and are focused on achieving those goals. Every student-athlete should be able to answer the following questions:

- Why do you want to play at this college/university?
- What do you plan to declare as your major?
- What are your plans for post-graduate life?
- What do you do in your spare time?
- Are you involved in your community?
- Do you have any questions?

The biggest mistake a student-athlete can make is to shrug and say, "I dunno," to any of these questions. Coaches want to recruit student-athletes who are focused on their future. Coaches are impressed with student-athletes who are motivated. Coaches look for student-athletes with determination and drive to achieve their goals. Those student-athletes are less likely to be a problem for the coach academically or in the community at large.

Majors, Minors, and Admission

Prior to a campus visit, student-athletes should spend some time on the school's website. Information regarding the various departments, degrees offered, and course requirements can be found online. Research the school. Take a virtual tour. If a student-athlete's desired major or minor is not offered at the school, the school may not be a good fit for the student-athlete.

Many colleges offer visits to campus that include sitting in on an actual class. The student-athlete should take advantage of this opportunity if it is available. After class, the student-athlete should make time to talk with the professor and/or the students to learn more about the school. This is an excellent time for the student-athlete to assess whether he or she will be able to juggle the demands of academics and athletics at the school.

While on campus, some schools will schedule an appointment with an admissions representative. In certain cases, admissions decisions can be made during the appointment. If this option is of interest to the student-athlete, the student-athlete will need to provide the admissions department with all necessary documents prior to the date of the visit.

After the Visit

Immediately after visiting a college campus the student-athlete should complete the following form. It is important to evaluate the school while the details are fresh because after a few visits, the campuses all tend to blur together. Grade the school on the various areas so you can compare it to other schools later.

QUESTIONS TO ASK WHILE ON YOUR COLLEGE VISIT

Academics
- ✓ How good is the department in my major?
- ✓ How many students are in each department?
- ✓ What is the typical class size?
- ✓ What credentials do the faculty members hold?
- ✓ What are the graduates of the program doing after they graduate?
- ✓ What percentage of scholarship athletes in my sport eventually graduate? In four years?
- ✓ What percentage of incoming students eventually graduate?
- ✓ What is the current team's average GPA?
- ✓ What academic support is given to student athletes?
- ✓ If I have a diagnosed and documented disability, what kind of academic services are available?
- ✓ How many credit hours should I take in season? How many outside of season?
- ✓ Are there restrictions on scheduling classes around practice?
- ✓ Is summer school available? If I go to summer school, will the university pay it for?

College Life
- ✓ What is a typical day for a student-athlete?
- ✓ What are the residence facilities like?
- ✓ Must student-athletes live on campus?

Financial Aid
- ✓ How much financial aid is available for summer school?
- ✓ What are the details of financial aid at your school?
- ✓ What would my scholarship cover?
- ✓ What can I receive in addition to the scholarship and how do I go about getting that?
- ✓ How long does my scholarship last? On what grounds can it be revoked?
- ✓ If I'm injured, what happens to my financial aid?
- ✓ What are my opportunities for employment while I'm a student-athlete?

College Evaluation Sheet

College A   College B   College C

_____   _____   _____

	Score from 1-10 (Dependant of Personal Preference - Ex. Distance From Home may be a 10 or 1 if the school is across the country dependant on if you want to go to school far away from home)		
Qualities	**College A**	**College B**	**College C**
College Size (# of Student/Size of Classes)			
College Setting (Rural, Urban, Suburban)			
Distance From Home			
Appearance (Town / School)			
Academic Area of Interest			
Prestige of the Athletic Programs			
Dorm/ Residence Facilities			
Food Options (Cafeteria/Off Campus)			
People at College (Are they people you'd like to be around for the next four years)			
Facilities and Buildings			
Social Life / Things to Do			

Total Score: _____   _____   _____

                 College A   College B   College C

Photo By M. Wegzyn

"You are never a loser until you quit trying."
Mike Ditka

Chapter 11

Camps and Showcases

Another way to catch a coach's attention is by attending certain camps and showcases. Some camps are better than others, and it is important to understand why this is so. Camps are often a means to boost a coach's income. Some camps are run by young players and are hardly more than babysitting experiences. Some camps actually are run by college and professional coaches and are the equivalent to a *school* for a particular sport. It is important to check into who will be running the camp.

Usually camps are beneficial to the student-athlete. Student-athletes receive instruction that will hone their skills from adult coaches who often coach at a neighboring college or are graduates of the school's athletic program. Sometimes, college coaches and other college recruiting companies scout these camps to look for prospective athletes.

Showcases are held in many sports. These showcases provide college coaches and scouts an opportunity to see large numbers of student-athletes at one time at one location. This can be very cost efficient for a recruiting coach, especially important to a coach limited by a small recruiting budget. Some of these showcases have costly entry fees and some may even require travel to another state, a hotel stay, etc. Please thoroughly check out any showcase a student-athlete is invited to attend. If the brochure lists names or schools of college coaches that are supposed to be attending the showcase, call the coaches' schools and verify the information. Some showcases are excellent opportunities for exposure, while others are great moneymakers for the organizer of the showcase.

Usually at these showcases, a number of coaches present are dressed in their school's colors and the name of the school and the mascot are displayed on their clothing. These coaches may run the various stations and interact with the student-athletes. While it is enjoyable to develop some level of camaraderie with those coaches during the event, those are sometimes not the only coaches evaluating the student-athlete. In the stands or off to one end of the showcase area there are any number of nondescript people who appear to be spectators or parents. These are often the coaches sent by various colleges to determine which student-athletes are of interest to their respective programs. These coaches normally do not carry a clipboard or dress in any fashion that would identify them as coaches. These coaches make discreet notes about certain student-athletes and match those athletes to the official listing of participants at a later time. When attending a showcase, it is important a student-athlete remembers to exhibit model behavior and to run out every drill every time, because coaches have eyes and ears everywhere.

Rivals, Scout, 24/7, and Other Recruiting Sites

Certain camps have an affiliation with some of the online recruiting reporting sites. This is important mainly for football and men's basketball. If a student-athlete attends a camp with one of these affiliations, the student-athlete may end up being listed on one of those sites. That is a very beneficial thing in the recruiting process. The other way to get listed on one of these sites is to receive a D1 scholarship offer.

Club, AAU, and Tournaments

Some sports do not recruit student-athletes based on high school sports accomplishments. In soccer and volleyball, for example, the club team may be where student-athletes get noticed. College coaches attend large prestigious tournaments to watch particular players, but often another player who was previously unknown to the coach is discovered. In addition, soccer players are selected for ODP, the Olympic Development Program. Participation in the ODP is another excellent way for college coaches to find a soccer player.

Basketball players often face the most intense competition in AAU (Amateur Athletic Union) leagues. Many AAU basketball teams travel to top tournaments in other states. College coaches from that area attend those tournaments to find players that may be a good fit for their school. From these tournaments, the top players are invited to basketball showcases. The showcases provide players with an additional opportunity to be noticed by college coaches.

Another place basketball players can play with and against other talented student-athletes and be exposed to college coaches is at a Five-Star Camp. Five-Star's website, www.five-starbasketball.com boasts that more players have received scholarships through the Five-Star Basketball System than any other organization in basketball. Five-Star has been around for years and is known as one of the best camps for serious basketball players.

Baseball and softball are other sports that depend on travel team exposure for college scholarship opportunities. Players can attend showcases organized by companies such as "Perfect Game". Stats from these showcases are distributed to college coaches.

If you aren't sure where college coaches look for prospective athletes in a particular sport, don't be afraid to call a few college coaches and ask. The greater the number of college coaches that see a student-athlete play, the more opportunities a student-athlete has to play his or her sport in college.

Schedules

If a student-athlete is really interested in a particular school or if there is a school that is particularly interested in your student-athlete, send the coach a copy of the student-athlete's game/competition schedule. If it is possible, many coaches will try to attend an event to personally take a look at a student-athlete if it is allowed by the school's governing athletic body. If a student-athlete is traveling out-of-state to a tournament or showcase, it is important for the student-athlete to contact the coaches of schools within a two-hour radius of the tournament. No matter how big or how small the school, coaches appreciate the opportunity to take a look at an athlete 'live and in person,' and a tournament situation gives coaches that chance. Be sure to give the coach the name of the team, the uniform colors, the student-athlete's name, number and position, and, if possible, the tournament game schedule. Of course, keep in mind that coaches may be in attendance to watch other players. Sometimes the intensity or level of play of one student-athlete catches a coach's eye while the coach's intention was to watch, evaluate, and rate someone else. It is always important for a student-athlete to play hard in tournament and showcase situations.

REMEMBER: Marketing and exposure of student-athletes is crucial in the college recruiting process!

Notes

Photo by C. Yassay

"Set your goals high and don't stop till you get there."
Bo Jackson

Chapter 12

Other Important Topics

Is the Student-Athlete *Really* Being Recruited?

So far, much time, effort, and expense has been dedicated to marketing the student-athlete, but the student-athlete is **not truly being recruited** until a coach makes a visit to the student-athlete's home or invites the student-athlete on an *official* campus visit. These visits are the best way to evaluate the coach, the coach's integrity, and philosophies. Campus visits are best for determining if the school will be a good match for the student-athlete. The NCAA allows member schools to pay for athletes to visit their campuses. Some other governing bodies, like the NAIA, do not. Be sure to ask what the rules are when speaking to coaches.

Highlights

In some sports, college coaches expect to receive a link to highlight film. Often this is the only way for an out-of-area coach to see the student-athlete in action, which can separate one prospective athlete from another. Most schools tape their games and high school coaches allow these to be borrowed and copied. A good highlight film will have approximately five minutes of highlights of the student-athlete's best plays from games. There is no need to add music or any sound to the highlight film because college coaches tend to watch film with the sound muted. The tape should begin with a close up of the student-athlete followed by screens with information such as age, weight, height, position, year in school, name of high school, and team colors. Do not forget to include the name of the school the student-athlete attends as well as contact information for the athlete's head coach.

If the student-athlete is not talented with film editing, a professional may be hired to create the highlight film. It is important to have an arrow or a circle around the student athlete prior to the start of each play so the college coach can readily identify the player to watch.

Many sites on the Internet are willing to post a student-athlete's highlight film. As long as you can provide the coach with a link that will take the coach directly to the highlights, it doesn't matter what site you use. Some parents have been able to capitalize on their student-athlete's highlight film by posting the highlights to the parent's YouTube account. If enough people click on the highlights to view them, the parent may be contacted asking if the site may place ads on the account. If this happens, this generates some income for the parent.

Game Film

When a coach wants to take a serious look at student-athlete who participates in a sport that relies on game film, the coach will request the film of a complete game. There is no need to mark the game film with an arrow or circle around the student-athlete. The coach usually gives this film to a Graduate Assistant Coach (GA) who will cut it up so only the plays the student-athlete is in are kept and watched. Coaches will evaluate the student-athlete's performance over the course of an entire game.

Highlight film shows only the best plays by a student-athlete but little can be hidden in a full game film. If the student-athlete doesn't compete hard or is lazy, it will show up in the film. A student-athlete's endurance level and attitude will also be exposed in game film. It is important to provide the college coach film of a game where the student-athlete played his or her best. Do keep in mind, though; the coach may also obtain game film from another school in the league or on the team's schedule to watch the student-athlete. There is no way to control this. The only things a student-athlete can do are play hard every play and always have exemplary sportsmanship on the field.

The Highly Recruited Student-Athlete or "Blue Chip"

"Blue Chip" student-athletes are those that are being highly recruited. These student-athletes receive national attention and are considered to be among the best at their position in their sport. What needs to be understood is that the student-athlete who is a "blue chip" may or may not actually be the best at their position in their sport, but this student-athlete marketed him or herself early and well. The "blue chip" contacted numerous college coaches, attended camps, combines, and showcases, and marketed their skills early and often and is reaping the rewards.

Student-athletes that are Blue Chips or are aggressively recruited have problems and issues that are very different from the average student-athlete. The highly recruited student-athletes' phones ring constantly. It is important to set guidelines by which the college coaches are asked to abide. This is only for student-athletes who are so bombarded with phone calls and contacts that these contacts infringe on or prohibit normal, everyday life.

In this situation, an adult, usually the student-athlete's parents should screen all telephone contact with the student-athlete. The parents should get the name of the caller, the school he or she represents and its location, and the caller's title (head coach, recruiting coach, etc.). The student-athlete and parents might want to add other screening questions to learn whether the caller has seen or met the student-athlete or if the caller plans to visit the student-athlete's home or school, etc.

Be sure to inform callers of the times and days the student-athlete will take phone calls. Set up a schedule that is convenient for the student-athlete. (It is important the student-athlete have time to do homework, work out, rest, etc.) If a schedule is not enforced, the student-athlete will spend every evening talking on the phone with coaches. Be firm with this schedule. If a coach does not respect the schedule, this may not be the best school for the student-athlete.

Phone calls from coaches need to have time limits. In other words, phone calls should be limited to 15 to 20 minutes. Some coaches will try to extend conversations with Blue Chip student-athletes so the student-athlete's line is tied up and the coach can monopolize the student-athlete's time. If the schedule allows calls Monday, Wednesday, and Friday from 4 to 6 p.m., every coach is going to attempt to phone the student-athlete during the same six hours each week. If calls are not limited to a designated length of time, the student-athlete's opportunity to speak with other coaches is limited or lost.

Be sure to document all phone calls. In the school's folder, note the date, time, and name of caller. Make notes of what was discussed during the call. This call log will help differentiate schools later.

Recruiting Periods and Rules Per Class in School

The NCAA has iron clad rules in place regarding when student-athletes may and may not be contacted. These dates change annually. It is difficult to keep up with the exact dates every year but these are all clearly listed and spelled out in the NCAA Guide for the College-Bound Student-Athlete. The publication is printed every year in November and should be referenced each and every year of a high school student-athlete's athletic career.

Finding the Right School for the Student-Athlete

Parents need to listen closely to their student-athletes during the college selection process. Some student-athletes may prefer an urban campus while others want an isolated campus community in the countryside. Sometimes parents have a vision in their head of the ideal school for their son or daughter and that vision is very different from the student-athlete's. Parents need to realize how influential they can be and not push their favorite school onto the student-athlete. Many student-athletes have gone to the school that was their parents' "dream school" only to realize later that it wasn't the ideal place for them and transfer out. If a student-athlete were to begin college at a small NCAA D2 school and then decide to transfer to a NCAA D1 school, the student-athlete would be subjected to the NCAA transfer rules and would have to sit out of a year's athletic competition.

Walk-On and Preferred Walk-On

Some student-athletes will not be offered an athletic scholarship. Instead, a walk-on or preferred walk-on position is offered. A preferred walk-on is someone who agrees to be a part of the team and will have a roster spot but receives no athletic aid or athletic scholarship money. A walk-on is someone who "walks on" the team and, in some cases, has to successfully survive a try-out in order to earn a spot on the team roster. Much of the time this offer comes with a promise of a future scholarship or the opportunity to possibly earn a scholarship at a later date based on the student-athlete's performance.

There are success stories and horror stories of student-athletes who have walked on to teams. Before such an offer is accepted, the student-athlete should check with other schools to see if an athletic scholarship might be awarded. Also, contacting schools in a lower division or looking into schools within another governing body's jurisdiction might result in an athletic scholarship for the student-athlete. Be certain to explore all the details prior to arriving on campus as a walk-on.

Early Enrollment

Some coaches regularly ask student-athletes if it is possible for them to graduate high school after the first semester of their senior year. This early graduation usually takes place in December. There is no graduation ceremony or fanfare for high school students that graduate early.

The coach will present a scenario to the student-athlete indicating that the student-athlete will get a jump ahead of all of the other student-athletes in his or her class by getting on campus early. During the months the early enrollee is on campus ahead of the rest of the class, he or she can be working out in the weight room, getting to know his or her teammates, and learning the plays, routines, and schedules of the team. This might give the student-athlete an opportunity to play sooner or even start sooner than an athlete that arrives on campus in July or August of that same year. This is all true and it is usually very enticing.

The points the coach will not make are that enrolling early will deprive the student-athlete with some life experiences that create lifelong memories. Attending senior prom, graduation with friends, end of the year activities, etc., all are events that cannot be redone. The other fact to consider is this; a 17 or 18 year-old student-athlete who enrolls early will be competing with and against 22 and 23 year old student-athletes. In a contact sport, this presents a huge mismatch in most cases.

Careful thought needs to be given to an early-enrollment offer. Do not make a hasty decision and be certain this is an offer that will be in the best interest of the student-athlete.

Head Count vs. Equivalency Sports

Some sports are "head count sports" and others are not. A "head count sport" is a sport where each scholarship recipient receives a full scholarship. The NCAA limits the numbers of student-athletes that can receive scholarships but each student-athlete who receives a scholarship, will get a full scholarship.

At the NCAA D1 level, head count sports include men's and women's basketball, football, women's volleyball and women's tennis.

All other sports are "equivalency sports". The NCAA limits the total financial aid that a school can offer in a given sport. The limit given by the NCAA differs by sport and is the equivalent of a set number of full scholarships. Each scholarship may be awarded in partial parts so that the greatest possible number of student-athletes may receive some shared aid. Each full scholarship may be given in whole or as a half, third or quarter of a whole scholarship.

It is Good to Have Options

Aggressive marketing of a student-athlete to a minimum of 100 schools in all divisions and athletic associations is the best way to gain an advantage in the recruiting process. If a student-athlete receives five offers from the 100 to 300 schools contacted, the student-athlete will have more bargaining power with each of the schools and might be able to help shape the offer that is accepted.

A student-athlete who puts all his eggs in one basket, so to speak, has less of a chance of winning an athletic scholarship. If a coach is certain a student-athlete will attend his or her college whether the student-athlete gets an athletic scholarship or not, a coach is more likely to offer that scholarship to an athlete the coach needs to win over.

Photo by M. Wegzyn

"**Defeat is not the worst of failures. Not to have tried is the true failure.**"

George E. Woodberry

Chapter 13

Offers and Financial Aid

A student-athlete must be able to be admitted to the school before a financial award can be offered. When a coach requests a student-athlete apply to his or her school, the admission application fee can sometimes be waived if the admission paperwork is sent directly to the coach rather than to the admissions office. After admission to the school has been granted, the school needs a number of forms before a financial aid package can be assembled. The most commonly requested form is the Free Application for Federal Student Aid (FAFSA).

FAFSA

Just like January 1ˢᵗ is New Year's Day, parents of college students should consider January 2ⁿᵈ to be FAFSA Day! Not completing this form is one of the biggest and most costly mistakes made by student-athletes and their parents. Without the data from the FAFSA, most colleges will not offer a student-athlete any type of scholarship or financial aid.

Many parents wait to complete the FAFSA until they receive their W-2 and 1099 forms from employers. This is a mistake. It is better to estimate the amount of income earned and submit the form because it can be revised at a later date when the correct figures are received.

What most people do not realize is that FAFSA submissions are queued in the order received. In other words, these are placed in line according to the submission dates. Even if you go back in and adjust some of the information the submission date remains the original submission date. Aid is awarded to students in the order that the FAFSA is received. A student with a FAFSA that is submitted in early January has a much greater chance of receiving aid than a student who's FAFSA is submitted in June. Even though the June student may qualify for aid, if all the aid has all been awarded for the year, the student will not receive aid.

Verbal Offers and Commitments

A verbal offer is "worth the paper it is written on". In other words, it is not binding. While most coaches are true to their word, occasionally a coach will make a verbal offer to a student-athlete and not honor it later in the recruiting process. A verbal offer can be withdrawn at any time. If a coach extends a verbal offer to a student-athlete and the student-athlete does not make a verbal commitment in return, the coach will most likely continue to recruit student-athletes for that position. Sometimes a coach will offer three student-athletes for every one scholarship spot available. The first student-athlete to verbally commit to the coach will get the spot and the other two are out of luck.

Making a verbal commitment to a coach is a difficult decision because, once a student-athlete is committed, some coaches from other schools will no longer recruit that student-athlete. Of course, some coaches pay no attention to verbal offers and will try to convince a student-athlete to change his or her mind and to switch allegiances. Student-athletes who have made verbal commitments are under no obligation to honor the commitment.

Offers

Until a student-athlete is presented with a written offer from a school, other colleges need to be considered. If a coach believes other schools are competing for the same student-athlete and that student-athlete is near the top of the coach's recruiting list or depth chart, the coach's college may offer additional financial incentives for the student-athlete to choose his or her program. If a coach believes a student-athlete has no other options, the coach may try to recruit the athlete for as little as possible and use the unused resources for another recruit who may be negotiating more effectively.

It is important to get all the details about the conditions of any financial aid package offered before making any commitments. Will the financial aid be available to the student-athlete if the athlete suffers injury and is unable to participate? If the student-athlete takes classes during the summer term, will tuition and fees be covered by the scholarship? How many years is the award guaranteed to be available to the student-athlete? If this is a one-year deal, what is the probability of having it extended? What would cause the student-athlete to lose this award?

Successfully negotiating a package of financial aid is a delicate process. The student-athlete and parents should be honest and try to maintain control of the process. In order to realize desired results, there are a few tips to remember. The parents and student-athlete must make coaches aware of the amount of financial aid award that is needed. Coaches must be informed that no commitment will be made unless a formal award letter or contract is presented. If an award is presented that is less than expected or needed, the student-athlete or the student-athlete's parents should not hesitate to tell the coach how much more is needed to secure a deal. If at any time any part of the package does not live up to needs, agreements, and/or expectations, the coach must be informed of the discrepancy. If a coach truly cannot offer a student-athlete any more aid, often an appointment will be set up for the student-athlete by the coach with a financial aid counselor at the school. Coaches know which financial aid counselors have had previous success at finding other funds that the student-athlete may be eligible to receive. Do not succumb to pressure or deadlines when negotiating a college financial aid package. Colleges will inform athletes of a cut-off date for new admissions. This date is rarely held fast and true. Students are admitted up until the first day of classes at most colleges and universities.

The very best advantage for a student-athlete is to be academically successful. If two athletes are similar in talent, a coach will always choose the academically superior athlete for the team because the coach will not have to worry about academic eligibility issues with that athlete. If athletic offers are less than needed, academic awards may be secured to increase the amount of the financial package. Academically successful student-athletes will qualify for admission to a greater number of schools, thus raising the number of opportunities to participate in college athletics.

Never lose sight of the goal, which is to have a college education fully or partially funded by participation in college athletics. Lifelong earning power is increased with a college degree. Student-athletes may capitalize on academic and athletic success by using those accomplishments to gain admission to the best college possible.

Signing Period/Signing Day

Every D1 and D2 NCAA sport has a day when National Letters of Intent are delivered to student-athletes. Some sports have early and late signing periods and others just have one signing period. A binding scholarship offer may not be made in writing prior to the first day of national signing day.

National Letter of Intent (NLI)

The National Letter of Intent, or NLI, is a program administered by the Collegiate Commissioners Association. The CCA was formed in 1939 to promote uniformity and standard treatment of issues in college sports. The NLI program, which began in 1964, reduces and limits recruiting pressure on student-athletes and preserves amateurism in college athletics. The program now includes more than 500 participating institutions.

By signing a NLI, a student-athlete agrees to attend the designated college or university of one academic year. In return, the participating institution agrees to provide athletic financial aid for one academic year) two semesters or three quarters) to the student-athlete, provided the student-athlete has gained admissions to the school and is a qualifier according to NCAA initial eligibility rules. Once a student-athlete has signed the NLI, participating institutions are prohibited from recruiting the student-athlete. A student-athlete may not sign more than one NLI.

The NLI is an agreement with the university – not with a particular coach or a particular sport. If the coach should leave the university, the student-athlete is still bound to the university due to the provisions in the NLI. The NLI is not a guarantee of playing time or a spot on the roster. A student-athlete is not required to sign a NLI but many do because it provides assurance of the stated athletic financial aid. Division III NCAA schools do not use the NLI because those schools do not offer athletic aid to student-athletes.

The NLI may be delivered to a student-athlete by expedited courier or express mail, email or fax machine. A NLI returned to the university by fax or electronically is valid. The NLI may not be hand delivered off campus to the student-athlete by a coach and a coach may not be present off campus when a student-athlete signs a NLI. Signing of a NLI may only occur during the official signing period. (Consult with www.nationalletter.org for designated signing periods for each sport.)

Prior to signing a NLI, a student-athlete and his or her parents should read the document in it entirety. Be sure to note what the school is offering. Is the offer a full or partial scholarship? It is important to know the total cost of attending the particular school so the student-athlete can compare this to the amount of the award. Any costs not spelled out in the NLI will be the student-athlete's responsibility.

The NLI can become null and void in certain situations. Please be sure to visit www.nationalletter.org for details and specifics and more information.

Walk-On and Preferred Walk-On

Some student-athletes will not be offered an athletic scholarship. Instead, a walk-on or preferred walk-on position is offered. A preferred walk-on is someone who agrees to be a part of the team and will have a roster spot but receives no athletic aid or athletic scholarship money. A walk-on is someone who "walks on" the team and, in some cases, has to successfully survive a try-out in order to earn a spot on the team roster. Much of the time this offer comes with a promise of a future scholarship or the opportunity to possibly earn a scholarship at a later date based on the student-athlete's performance.

There are success stories and horror stories of student-athletes who have walked on to teams. Before such an offer is accepted, the student-athlete should check with other schools to see if an athletic scholarship might be awarded. Also, contacting schools in a lower division or looking into schools within another governing body's jurisdiction might result in an athletic scholarship for the student-athlete. Be certain to explore all the details prior to arriving on campus as a walk-on.

Early Enrollment

Some coaches regularly ask student-athletes if it is possible for them to graduate high school after the first semester of their senior year. This early graduation usually takes place in December. There is no graduation ceremony or fanfare for high school students that graduate early.

The coach will present a scenario to the student-athlete indicating that the student-athlete will get a jump ahead of all of the other student-athletes in his or her class by getting on campus early. During the months the early enrollee is on campus ahead of the rest of the class, he or she can be working out in the weight room, getting to know his or her teammates, and learning the plays, routines, and schedules of the team. This might give the student-athlete an opportunity to play sooner or even start sooner than an athlete that arrives on campus in July or August of that same year. This is all true and it is usually very enticing.

The points the coach will not make are that enrolling early will deprive the student-athlete with some life experiences that create lifelong memories. Attending senior prom, graduation with friends, end of the year activities, etc., all are events that cannot be redone. The other fact to consider is this; a 17 or 18 year-old student-athlete who enrolls early will be competing with and against 22 and 23 year old student-athletes. In a contact sport, this presents a huge mismatch in most cases.

Careful thought needs to be given to an early-enrollment offer. Do not make a hasty decision and be certain this is an offer that will be in the best interest of the student-athlete.

Head count vs. Equivalency Sports

Some sports are "head count sports" and others are not. A "head count sport" is a sport where each scholarship recipient receives a full scholarship. The NCAA limits the numbers of student-athletes that can receive scholarships but each student-athlete who receives a scholarship gets a full scholarship.

At the NCAA D1 level, head count sports include men's and women's basketball, football, women's volleyball and women's tennis.

All other sports are "equivalency sports". The NCAA limits the total financial aid that a school can offer in a given sport. The limit given by the NCAA differs by sport and is the equivalent of a set number of full scholarships. Each scholarship may be awarded in partial parts so that the greatest possible number of student-athletes may receive some shared aid. Each full scholarship may be given in whole or as a half, third or quarter of a whole scholarship.

Length of Scholarship

Athletic scholarships are awarded for a one-year period of time. The terms, "full-ride" or "four-year package", are technically inaccurate. Many coaches make the promise that an athletic scholarship will be renewed all four years of a student-athlete's eligibility during the recruiting process. Many of these coaches honor their word – some do not. Some student-athletes are forced to renegotiate athletic financial aid packages each and every year. Researching the recruiting habits and history of each coach, team, and school can help eliminate such unpleasant surprises.

Photo by Steve Fecht

"Football doesn't build character, it reveals it."
Marv Levy

Chapter 14

Social Media/Your Personal Brand

Brand insignias are everywhere and whether we realize it or not, we have perceptions about certain brands. If someone saw a Cadillac logo, they may think of luxury cars. McDonald's golden arches might invoke thoughts of fast food, grease, and cheap. Large companies do everything to protect their brand and to have consumers associate their brands with something positive.

Student-athletes also have brands. These brands are called by different names such as reputation, character, position, and standing-in-the-community to name a few. Every person has a brand and college coaches will try to discover what a student-athlete's brand is prior to offering an athletic scholarship. It is important for a college coach to learn what a student-athlete is all about because the coach has to decide if he or she wants to spend the next four or five years in a close relationship with this person. Also, the coach needs to decide if the student-athlete is likely to bring honor or shame to the team and the school.

Before a scholarship offer is made a college coach will ask a student-athlete's high school coaches and club coaches about the student-athlete's character. If a student-athlete has gotten into trouble at the school or with the local authorities, college coaches will discover this and it will hurt the student-athlete's recruitment opportunities.

Social Media

High school students don't realize the impact of social media on their lives and their futures. In this "information age", there is a record of everything one texts, posts, tweets, blogs, etc. Thirty years from now when today's high school student-athletes are having children of their own and holding down full-time jobs, their photos and words posted in high school could come back to haunt them. Baby boomers are fortunate because all of the crazy things they did during their high school years were not documented. Tall tales can be told about walking to school, barefoot and in the snow, uphill both ways!

Who Sees What You Post?

High school students tend to be trusting. When offered a "Friend Request", most will accept without giving much thought about it. The photo of the person requesting access to all of their posts and pictures appears to be a peer. In reality, that new cute new 17 year-old girl might be a 54 year-old man who coaches offensive line at a college or university. It could also be a college admissions officer. Both are using this type of stealth technique to learn about potential students and student-athletes.

Student-athletes need to go through all of their social media accounts and remove anything that might hurt their "brand" or reputation. Nothing should be "out there" that they wouldn't be proud to have their church-going grandmother or, eventually, their own children see or read.

"On-the-Field" Brand

Another thing for student-athletes to consider is, what is their "On-the-Field" brand? Is the student-athlete known for not playing hard when the play isn't coming their way? Do they quit halfway back up the court when their team is on defense? Perhaps the student-athlete is known to be injury prone or "soft". Some student-athletes are known for temper tantrums – student-athletes who are known for screaming, swearing, and/or throwing things during a contest are not desirable by college coaches.

When recruiting athletes in sports where there is game film, a college coach will watch entire games to see how a student-athlete performs over the length of the competition. While the coach or student-athlete will provide game film that puts the student-athlete in a complimentary light, it is easy for college coaches to get film from other schools in the league in which the student-athlete's team plays. There was a case of a wide receiver that didn't get recruited because of some things coaches saw him do on another team's game film.

Your Brand is Built Everywhere You Go

Student-athletes often believe that the things they do off the school grounds or when not with the team will remain unknown to others. This is not the case. It is also a fallacy to believe that good behavior isn't necessary when no coach is around.

It is especially important to protect your brand when attending camps and showcases. There are high school student-athletes who attend these events every weekend and are seen by alumni players of colleges. Those former players have a direct line to the head coaches and position coaches of their school and, often, many others. One phone call from these former players can make or break the recruitment of a high school student-athlete.

What is your brand? Be certain you control it and it reflects you in a positive way!

GLOSSARY OF TERMS

Amateurism – As of 2006, if a student-athlete plans to participate in intercollegiate athletics at an NCAA Division I or II institution in fall 2007 or thereafter, the student-athlete must have his or her amateur status certified by the NCAA Eligibility Center.

Contact – A contact is any face-to-face contact between a coach and a student-athlete or a student-athlete's parent(s) off the college's campus involving anything more than "hello." A contact also occurs if a coach has any contact with you or your parent(s) at your high school or any location where you are competing or practicing.

Contact Period – A designated period of time when a college coach may have in-person contact with a prospective student-athlete and/or the student-athlete's parent(s) on or off the college's campus, watch a student-athlete play, visit a student-athlete's high school, write and/or telephone a student-athlete. A student-athlete and the student-athlete's parent(s) may visit a college campus during this time.

Cost of Attendance – An amount calculated by a school's financial-aid office using federal regulations. This amount includes the total cost of tuition, fees, room, board, books, supplies, transportation, and other expenses related to attendance at the school.

Counter – A student, who is receiving financial aid from a school, who counts toward the maximum number of scholarships allowed in a sport.

Core Courses – Academic courses that meet criteria dictated by the NCAA.

Dead Period – A designated period of time during which college coaches may not have any in-person contact with a prospective student-athlete or the student-athlete's parent(s). During this time a college coach may write and telephone a student-athlete and/or a student-athlete's parent(s).

Division I – An NCAA classification, Division I member institutions have to sponsor at least seven sports for men and seven for women (or six for men and eight for women) with two team sports for each gender. Each playing season has to be represented by each gender as well. There are contest and participant minimums for each sport, as well as scheduling criteria. For sports other than football and basketball, Division I schools must play 100 percent of the minimum number of contests against Division I opponents -- anything over the minimum number of games has to be 50 percent Division I. Men's and women's basketball teams have to play all but two games against Division I teams; for men, they must play one-third of all their contests in the home arena. Schools that have football are classified as Division I FBS (formerly I-A) or Division I FCS (formerly I-AA). Division I FBS football schools usually are fairly elaborate programs. Division I FBS teams has to meet minimum attendance requirements (average 15,000 people in actual or paid attendance per home game), which must be met once in a rolling two-year period. Division I FCS teams do not need to meet minimum attendance requirements. Division I schools must meet minimum financial aid awards for their athletics program, and there are maximum financial aid awards for each sport that a Division I school cannot exceed.

Division II – An NCAA classification, Division II institutions have to sponsor at least five sports for men and five for women, (or four for men and six for women), with two team sports for each gender, and each playing season represented by each gender. There are contest and participant minimums for each sport, as well as scheduling criteria -- football and men's and women's basketball teams must play at least 50% of their games against Division II or Division I FBS or Division I FCS opponents. For sports other than football and basketball there are no scheduling requirements. There are not attendance requirements for football or arena game requirements for basketball. There are maximum financial aid awards for each sport that a Division II school must not exceed. Division II teams usually feature a number of local or in-state student-athletes. Many Division II student-athletes pay for school through a combination of scholarship money, grants, student loans and employment earnings. Division II athletics programs are financed in the institution's budget like other academic departments on campus. Traditional rivalries with regional institutions dominate schedules of many Division II athletics programs.

Division III – an NCAA classification, Division III colleges and universities may not offer athletic scholarships, which does not mean that financial aid is not awarded to student-athletes; Division III schools do not use the NCAA Clearinghouse for eligibility; Division III institutions have to sponsor at least five sports for men and five for women, with two team sports for each gender, and each playing season represented by each gender. There are minimum contest and participant minimums for each sport. Division III athletics features student-athletes who receive no financial aid related to their athletic ability and athletic departments are staffed and funded like any other department in the university. Division III athletics departments place special importance on the impact of athletics on the participants rather than on the spectators. The student-athlete's experience is of paramount concern. Division III athletics encourages participation by maximizing the number and variety of athletics opportunities available to students, placing primary emphasis on regional in-season and conference competition.

Eligibility – Meeting the stipulated requirements to participate and compete in college athletics.

Evaluation – An activity by a coach to assess a prospective student-athlete's academic or athletic ability, this may include visiting a student-athlete's high school and watching a student-athlete practice or compete.

Evaluation Period – A period of time during which a college coach is permitted to write, telephone and/or watch a prospective student-athlete play or visit a student-athlete's high school, but the coach may not have any in-person conversations with the student-athlete or the student-athlete's parents off the college's campus. The student-athlete may visit a college campus during this period.

Four-Year Full-Ride Athletic Scholarship – A fallacy. Refers to a four-year scholarship that covers all costs associated with a college education, such as tuition, fees, books, room, and board. NCAA athletic scholarships are limited to one year and are renewed annually. There is no such award as a four-year full-ride athletic scholarship.

Full grant-in-aid – Financial aid that consists of tuition, fees, room, board, and required course books. Often referred to as a full-ride.

Grant – A form of financial aid that does not have to be repaid.

Initial Counter – A student who is receiving countable institutional financial aid in a sport for the first time.

Initial Eligibility – See NCAA Eligibility Center.

Institutional Aid – All financial aid administered by the college or university. This includes, but is not limited to, any scholarship, grant, tuition waiver, or loan. It also includes any financial aid from the government or private sources if the school is responsible for selecting the recipient or determining the amount of aid.

Loan – A form of financial aid that must be repaid with interest at a predetermined date in the future.

NAIA – National Association of Intercollegiate Athletics; the governing body in college athletics for nearly 300 colleges and universities in 25 conferences and 14 regions across the U.S. and Canada offering 23 championships in 13 sports. www.naia.org

National Letter of Intent – A voluntary program administered by the Collegiate Commissioners Association, not by the NCAA; an agreement signed by a student-athlete agreeing to attend an institution for one year in exchange for one year's athletic financial aid. www.national-letter.org

NCAA – National Collegiate Athletic Association. The governing body for more than 1,280 colleges, universities, conferences and organizations. It develops rules and guidelines for athletics eligibility and athletics competition for each of the three NCAA divisions. www.NCAA.org

NCAA Initial Eligibility Clearinghouse – Officially known as the NCAA Eligibility Center. Also known as "the clearinghouse" and "NCAA Eligibility Clearinghouse." The Clearinghouse is defunct as of 2007 and has been replaced by the NCAA Eligibility Center. Students who want to participate in D-I and D-II college sports during their first year of enrollment in college MUST register with the Eligibility Center.

NCAA Eligibility Center – The new department of the NCAA that will handle all eligibility and amateurism issues in order to qualify for participation in NCAA athletics.

NCCAA – National Christian College Athletic Association. The governing body for over 100 Christian colleges nationwide, both liberal arts and Bible colleges. www.thenccaa.org

NJCAA – National Junior College Athletic Association. The governing body in junior college athletics for more than 500 schools. www.njcaa.org

NLI – See National Letter of Intent.

Nonqualifier – A student-athlete who does not meet the academic requirements of the NCAA for eligibility. There are different eligibility qualifications for D-I and D-II schools.

Official Visit – Any visit to a college campus by a prospective student-athlete and/or a student-athlete's parent(s) that is paid for by the college. Funds may be provided to pay for transportation to and from the college, lodging and meals (three per day) while visiting the college, reasonable entertainment expenses including three complimentary admissions to a home athletics contest. Prior to an Official Visit, the student-athlete must provide the college with a copy of a high school transcript (D-I only), and SAT, ACT, or PLAN score. "Official Visits" are allowed beginning the first day of classes of a student-athlete's senior year in high school; student-athletes are limited to a maximum of five "official visits" to D-I and D-II colleges.

Partial Scholarship – A scholarship that does not cover all college costs, but does cover some expenses. A "partial scholarship" may cover the cost of any but not all of the following: Tuition, fees, books, room, board; this is the most common college scholarship awarded to student-athletes.

Period of the Award – The period of the award begins on the first day of classes for a semester or quarter, or the first day of practice, whichever comes first. The period of award ends at the conclusion of the period set forth in the financial aid agreement, which is usually the last day of classes for a semester or quarter. The grant-in-aid may not be awarded for more than one academic year.

Prospect – See Prospective Student-Athlete.

Prospective Student-Athlete – You become a "prospective student-athlete" when you start ninth-grade classes, or before ninth-grade when a college gives you, your relatives, or your friends any financial aid or other benefits that the college does not provide to students generally.

Qualifier – A student-athlete who meets the academic requirements of the NCAA. There are different eligibility qualifications for eligibility for D-I and D-II schools.

Quiet Period – A period of time during which college coaches may not: 1) have any in-person contact with a prospective student-athlete or student-athlete's parent(s) off the college's campus; 2) watch a student-athlete play; 3) visit a student-athlete's high school. College coaches may write or telephone a student-athlete during this time, and a student-athlete and the student-athlete's parent(s) may visit a college campus during this time.

Recruiting Calendars – A list of dates that are designated as a "contact period," "dead period," "evaluation period," or "quiet period." There is a different recruiting calendar for each NCAA sport. To look at calendars for all sports go to www.ncaa.org.

Recruiting Companies - Consultants who, for a fee, compile profiles on student-athletes with the purpose of marketing those student-athletes to colleges.

Red Shirt Freshman - Some first-year students are given the "red-shirt" designation by a college coach which means the student-athlete participated in a college's academic year but did not participate during that year's sports season. Usually a "red-shirt freshman" is a sophomore in college who practiced with the team during the first year of academic enrollment at the school but did not play in any games (at the coach's request), or was seriously injured during the first season. The "red-shirt" designation means that that season will not count against the player's four years of NCAA eligibility, allowing the student-athlete to play four full seasons.

Scholarship – A type of financial aid awarded to a student that does not have to be repaid.

Sliding Scale – A scale that determines a student-athlete's eligibility for Division I college athletics based on Core GPA and ACT/SAT test scores. (There is no sliding scale in Division-II.)

Test Score Sliding Scale – A scale that determines a student-athlete's eligibility for Division I college athletics based on Core GPA and ACT/SAT test scores. (There is no sliding scale in Division-II.)

True Freshman - A freshman athlete who is playing for a school during his or her first year of college classes.

Unofficial Visit – Any self-funded visit by a prospective student-athlete and a student-athlete's parents to a college campus. The only expense the college may pay for is tickets for three admissions to a home athletics contest. A student-athlete and a student-athlete's parents may make an "Unofficial Visit" at any time and the number of "Unofficial Visits" that may be made by a student-athlete is unlimited. If an "Unofficial Visit" is made to a campus during a "Dead Time," the coach is not permitted to talk with the student-athlete or the student-athlete's parent(s).

USCAA – United States College Athletic Association, formerly the National Small College Athletic Association. The governing body in athletics for more than 100 small-school athletic programs.

Visit – See "Official Visit" and "Unofficial Visit."

Walk On – A college athlete who is not recruited to play a particular sport but attends a general tryout and makes the team. Walk on athletes do not receive any financial aid even though the college may award athletic scholarships to other athletes on the team.

CONTACT INFORMATION

NCAA

The National Collegiate Athletic Association
700 W. Washington Street
P.O. Box 6222
Indianapolis, Indiana 46206-6222
Phone: 317/917-6222
Fax: 317/917-6888
For students and parents with eligibility questions:
NCAA Eligibility Center
877/262-1492
(Toll free) 317/223-0700

NCAA Eligibility Center

Transcript/Document Mailing Address:
NCAA Eligibility Center - Certification Processing
P.O. Box 7136
Indianapolis, IN 46207

Overnight/Express Mailing Address:
NCAA Eligibility Center - Certification Processing
1802 Alonzo Watford Sr. Drive
Indianapolis, IN 46202

NCAA - National Collegiate Athletic Association Guide

www.ncaa.org
NCAA Publications
(Request "Guide to the College-Bound Student-Athlete")
1-800-638-3731
317-917-6222
Customer Service (M-F, noon – 4 pm Eastern time)
P.O. Box 6222
Indianapolis, IN 46206-6222

NAIA - National Association of Intercollegiate Athletics
www.naia.org
www.championsofcharacter.org

NAIA Eligibility Center Offices
Phone: 816-595-8300
Toll free: 866-881-6242
Fax: 816-595-8301
Email: ecinfo@naia.org
International student questions, contact: ecinternational@naia.org

Transcript & Fee Waiver Confirmation Address:
NAIA Eligibility Center
P.O. Box 15340
Kansas City, MO 64106

Office Location:
1200 Grand Blvd., Suite 100
Kansas City, MO 64106

Business Hours:
Monday through Friday 8:30 am to 5 pm Central

NCCAA - National Christian College Athletic Association
www.thenccaa.org
864-250-1199
302 W. Washington Street
Greenville, SC 29601
Phone: 864-250-1199
Fax: 864-250-1141
Office hours: M 9am-5pm, T-F 8:30am-5pm

NJCAA – National Junior College Athletic Association
www.njcaa.org
1631 Mesa Ave Suite B
Colorado Springs, CO 80906
Phone: 719-590-9788
Fax: 719-590-7324

USCAA – United States Collegiate Athletic Association Nation

www.theuscaa.com
739 Thimble Shoals Blvd. Suite 1011-E
Newport News, VA 23606
Phone: 757-706-3756 or 757-706-3757
Fax: 757-706-3758

CIS – Canadian Interuniveristy Sport

www.cis-sic.ca
801 King Edward, Suite N205
Ottawa, Ontario Canada K1N 6N5
Phone: 613-562-5670
Fax: 613-562-5669

CCAA – Canadian Collegiate Athletic Association

www.ccaa.ca
2 St. Lawrence Drive
Cornwall, Ontario Canada K6H 4Z1
Phone: 613-937-1508   Extension 1